Life in Napoleon's Army

The Napoleonic Library

Other books in the series include:

1815: THE RETURN OF NAPOLEON
Paul Britten Austin

ON THE FIELDS OF GLORY
The Battlefields of the 1815 Campaign
Andrew Uffindell and Michael Corum

DECLINE AND FALL OF NAPOLEON'S EMPIRE
How the Emperor Self-Destructed
Digby Smith

THE MEMOIRS OF BARON VON MÜFFLING
A Prussian Officer in the Napoleonic Wars
Baron von Müffling

WATERLOO LECTURES
A Study of the Campaign of 1815
Colonel Charles Chesney

WATERLOO LETTERS
A Collection of Accounts From Survivors of the Campaign of 1815
Edited by Major-General H. T. Siborne

www.frontline-books.com/napoleoniclibrary

Life in Napoleon's Army

The Graphic Memoirs of Captain Elzéar Blaze

Introduction by
Philip Haythorthwaite

Commentary by
Charles James Napier

Frontline Books

Life in Napoleon's Army

A Greenhill Book

Published in 1995 by Greenhill Books, Lionel Leventhal Limited
www.greenhillbooks.com

This edition published in 2015
and reprinted in this format in 2022 by

Frontline Books
an imprint of Pen & Sword Books Ltd,
47 Church Street, Barnsley, S. Yorkshire, S70 2AS
For more information on our books, please visit
www.frontline-books.com, email info@frontline-books.com
or write to us at the above address.

Copyright © Lionel Leventhal Limited, 1995

ISBN: 9-781-39901-970-5

All rights reserved. No part of this publication may be reproduced, stored in or introduced into a retrieval system, or transmitted, in any form, or by any means (electronic, mechanical, photocopying, recording or otherwise) without the prior written permission of the publisher. Any person who does any unauthorized act in relation to this publication may be liable to criminal prosecution and civil claims for damages.

CIP data records for this title are available from the British Library

Publishing History
Captain Elzéar Blaze's Memoirs were first published as *La Vie Militaire Sous Le Premier Empire Ou Moeurs De Garnison, Du Bivouac et De La Caserne* (Paris, 1837) and were published in English as part of *Lights and Shades of Military Life*, edited by Lt-Gen Charles James Napier (London 1850). This current edition presents the complete text from *Lights and Shades*, with additional illustrations by Job from *La Vie Militaire*, and an Introduction by Philip Haythornthwaite.

Printed and bound by 4edge Limited, UK

CONTENTS

Introduction by Philip Haythornthwaite vii

Chapter I: The Velites, and the Military School of Fontainebleau 1
  Editor's Remarks 13

Chapter II: The Bivouac and Marauders 19
  Editor's Remarks 36

Chapter III: Marches 37
  Editor's Remarks 63

Chapter IV: Quarters – Germany, Poland 69
  Editor's Remarks 93

Chapter V: Quarters – Spain 95

Chapter VI: A Day of Battle 115

Chapter VII: The Camp 143

Chapter VIII: The Garrison 152

Chapter IX: Barracks 162

Chapter X: Reviews 174

Chapter XI: Military Executions 189

INTRODUCTION

Elzéar Blaze, the author of this most attractive memoir of the Napoleonic Wars, was born at Cavaillon in 1787, the son of a lawyer, Henri Sébastien Blaze. He entered Napoleon's army as a youth, via the *Vélite* organization of the Imperial Guard, a path to commissioned rank open only to those of some wealth. After gaining his commission as an officer, he served in the campaigns of the empire from shortly after the Battle of Eylau until the conclusion of the Napoleonic Wars, attaining the rank of captain in 1814. He continued to serve after the Bourbon restoration, and only retired to Chénevières-sur-Marne after the revolution of 1830, to pursue his love of hunting. His military memoirs, *La Vie Militaire sous le Premier Empire, ou Mœurs de Garnison, du Bivouac et de la Caserne*, were published in 1837. Unlike many contemporary memoirists, Blaze did not devote this work to a chronological record of his own career, but rather to the character, customs and mode of operation of the French army at this most significant period, on the battlefield, in barracks, camp and boudoir, exemplified and enlivened by his own experiences and reminiscences.

That he was especially suited to produce such a work is demonstrated by the extent of his service. As a *Vélite* he experienced aspects of the life of the rank-and-file, and of service in the Imperial Guard; and later saw the army from a different viewpoint as an officer of the line. His active service was wide, from 1807 to 1815, in Poland, Germany and the Tyrol, in the Peninsular War and 'War of Liberation', as a witness to the conference at Tilsit and a participant in many of the epic battles of the period. Wagram is mentioned especially, although Blaze admitted, with a candour remarkable for the period, that the best battle he ever witnessed was Bautzen, for the fact that he watched it through his telescope from a church steeple, in safety! Blaze's own service also permitted him, presumably from conversations with veterans, to recount significant incidents from campaigns as early as that in the Vendée. The result is a valuable commentary upon the character and characteristics of the French soldier in the age of Napoleon; as described in the editorial preface to the first English edition, Blaze's pages include 'admirable descriptions of military life, and do credit to the wit and abilities of the author'.

Some explanation is required for the inclusion, in the present edition, of the editorial commentary which appears after each of the first four chapters. These comments were made by the editor of the first English edition, one of the most remarkable British soldiers of the mid-nineteenth century, Lieutenant-General Sir Charles James Napier (1782–1853), brother of the author of the classic history of the Peninsular War, and probably the most distinguished member of the renowned Napier family.

Charles Napier was commissioned into the British Army at the age of twelve, but was permitted to complete his schooling before embarking upon his military career. He served as a regimental officer during the Napoleonic Wars, most notably at Corunna, where as a major in the 50th (West Kent) Regiment he was wounded and captured. Incapacitated by his injuries, Napier was about to be killed by an Italian member of the French army when his life was saved by a French drummer named Guibert, who refused to permit the insult to the honour of his nation which would have resulted from the murder of a helpless enemy. This, and the caring and courteous treatment Napier received subsequently from the French Marshals Soult and Ney (especially the latter, who facilitated Napier's early release from captivity), led him to hold the French nation, its army, and Napoleon himself, in the highest regard. After further campaigning against the French (and sustaining a severe wound at Busaco), Charles Napier was appointed Inspecting Field Officer at Corfu in 1819, and from 1822 was governor of Cephalonia. Upon his resignation following one of his many clashes with authority, it appeared that Napier's military career had ended, and he devoted himself to literary pursuits (from which period came his edition of Blaze's work), until in 1839 he was appointed to command the Northern District. In September 1842 he was sent to India, where at a comparatively advanced age he began a most successful career as a commanding general in the field, winning immortal fame by his victories of Miani and Hyderabad, and the resulting British conquest of Sind.

Napier's edition of Blaze's memoir was published under the title *Lights and Shades of Military Life,* combined with Alfred de Vigny's better-known *Servitude et grandeur militaires,* which appeared in Napier's edition as *Recollections of Military Servitude* and *Recollections of Military Greatness.* Blaze's narrative in Napier's edition was entitled *Military Life in Bivouac, Camp, Garrison, Barracks, &c.* The stated purpose of Napier's comments was to provide a comparison between British and French soldiers, partly as an assistance to young British officers who might study the work; but their significance is now historical, rather than practical.

The thoughts of so distinguished a military commander are obviously of interest in themselves – not least his opinions on military history as written by civilians, given in the commentary to Chapter I. His admiration of the French army is obvious, although it was a somewhat idealized view (apparent, for example, in his doubts over the complicity of French officers in the process of looting). Elements of Napier's personal philosophy are also evident in his commentary; throughout his life, his political views were of a Radical and humanitarian complexion, although his dismissal of republicanism as 'contrary to nature' could hardly be clearer. Most notable, perhaps, are Napier's remarks upon British colonial policy in his commentary to Chapter III; yet only a few years after this was written, Napier was himself conducting a campaign in Sind which at the time was criticized in some quarters as being the least justified appropriation of territory undertaken by the British in India.

The current work reproduces the second edition of Napier's translation, published by Henry Colburn of London in 1850, and although most of Napier's preface has been omitted as being concerned largely with de Vigny's work, the following deserves inclusion:

'With regard to the translation, I shall not make any other remark than that I am no way answerable for its correctness or language; the praise or blame that merits belongs to the translator, on whom I should be sorry to commit any trespass, especially as I have no doubt that he understands French much better than myself. If, in my reveries, I have been stupid and prosy, I am sorry for it; but the reader has the remedy in his hands. Few men read observations and notes, so the former may skip over the "*Editor's*" dull notes and lose very little; for the small merit they contain is like a bad gold mine, and will not, I fear, repay the trouble of working. After this honest confession, I consider that all accounts of conscience between myself and the reader are clear.

C. J. Napier'.

The illustrations in the present edition are reproduced from a French edition of *La Vie Militaire sous le Premier Empire*, and are drawings by 'Job' (Jacques Onfroy de Bréville, 1858–1931), one of the greatest of historical book-illustrators, whose carefully researched work, even though not contemporary, captures the period and spirit of the troops of Napoleon's army.

Philip Haythornthwaite,
1995

CHAPTER I.

THE VELITES, AND MILITARY SCHOOL OF FONTAINEBLEAU.

In the time of the Empire, there were three ways of entering the military service: by entering as a private soldier, the simplest and the least costly; by enrolling one's self in the Velites; or by obtaining admission as a pupil into the military school of Fontainebleau.

Had Napoleon, when he instituted the Velites of the Imperial Guard, required only physical conditions in order to be admitted into this new corps, he would have found few applicants; but the decree of institution insisted that the young candidates should have had a certain education, and that each should pay a premium of two hundred francs in the infantry, and three hundred in the cavalry, merely to have the honour of being a soldier in the guard, with the promise of being made an officer at the expiration of four years. Applications poured in *en masse* to the ministry of war, and all the places were soon taken.

Philip Augustus was the first king of France who constituted a body of picked men to guard his person. Being one day informed that the sheik, commonly called the Old Man of the Mountain, had formed a plan for assassinating him, he immediately assembled his brave nobility, and selected one hundred gentlemen, whom he armed with maces of brass, bows and arrows, and ordered to attend him wherever he went: they were called sergeants-at-arms. Such was the origin of the first guard of our kings; hence arose the body guard, the imperial guard, and the royal guard.

At the commencement of the present century, martial ideas were fermenting in all young heads, and the glorious exploits of our armies filled and made every heart throb with noble enthusiasm. Themistocles of old could not sleep for thinking of the triumphs of Miltiades. Ambition, that mighty motive of human actions, which is frequently confounded with love of country, propelled all the young men of twenty towards our distant frontiers: perhaps, too, the prospects of the inevitable conscription induced them to enrol themselves beforehand; just as a swimmer, seeing a storm approaching, puts his clothes under cover, and throws himself into the river.

The ranks of the army were always ready to receive a new comer; the ranks being thinned from time to time by the cannon, vacant places were constantly to be found; but the knapsack, the musket, and life in barracks, were much more dreaded by the young men, tenderly brought up, than balls and bullets. This noviciate might last very long, nay, it might last for ever; for was any one certain of surmounting the hardships, of being able to do as well or better than others?—these conditions being rigorously enforced, in order to qualify for officer.

The military school of Fontainebleau threw open its doors for twelve hundred francs per annum; but, being beset by a crowd of young men, all could not pass them. Those who had not time to wait their turn for admission entered into the Velites: it was a more toilsome life; the epaulet was attained with greater difficulty, but the uniform was sooner donned, and at eighteen that is something. None but a soldier of that period can conceive what a spell there was in the uniform. What lofty expectations inflamed all the young heads on which a plume of feathers waved for the first time!

CHAPTER I.

THE VELITES, AND MILITARY SCHOOL OF FONTAINEBLEAU.

In the time of the Empire, there were three ways of entering the military service: by entering as a private soldier, the simplest and the least costly; by enrolling one's self in the Velites; or by obtaining admission as a pupil into the military school of Fontainebleau.

Had Napoleon, when he instituted the Velites of the Imperial Guard, required only physical conditions in order to be admitted into this new corps, he would have found few applicants; but the decree of institution insisted that the young candidates should have had a certain education, and that each should pay a premium of two hundred francs in the infantry, and three hundred in the cavalry, merely to have the honour of being a soldier in the guard, with the promise of being made an officer at the expiration of four years. Applications poured in *en masse* to the ministry of war, and all the places were soon taken.

Philip Augustus was the first king of France who constituted a body of picked men to guard his person. Being one day informed that the sheik, commonly called the Old Man of the Mountain, had formed a plan for assassinating him, he immediately assembled his brave nobility, and selected one hundred gentlemen, whom he armed with maces of brass, bows and arrows, and ordered to attend him wherever he went: they were called sergeants-at-arms. Such was the origin of the first guard of our kings; hence arose the body guard, the imperial guard, and the royal guard.

At the commencement of the present century, martial ideas were fermenting in all young heads, and the glorious exploits of our armies filled and made every heart throb with noble enthusiasm. Themistocles of old could not sleep for thinking of the triumphs of Miltiades. Ambition, that mighty motive of human actions, which is frequently confounded with love of country, propelled all the young men of twenty towards our distant frontiers: perhaps, too, the prospects of the inevitable conscription induced them to enrol themselves beforehand; just as a swimmer, seeing a storm approaching, puts his clothes under cover, and throws himself into the river.

The ranks of the army were always ready to receive a new comer; the ranks being thinned from time to time by the cannon, vacant places were constantly to be found; but the knapsack, the musket, and life in barracks, were much more dreaded by the young men, tenderly brought up, than balls and bullets. This noviciate might last very long, nay, it might last for ever; for was any one certain of surmounting the hardships, of being able to do as well or better than others?—these conditions being rigorously enforced, in order to qualify for officer.

The military school of Fontainebleau threw open its doors for twelve hundred francs per annum; but, being beset by a crowd of young men, all could not pass them. Those who had not time to wait their turn for admission entered into the Velites: it was a more toilsome life; the epaulet was attained with greater difficulty, but the uniform was sooner donned, and at eighteen that is something. None but a soldier of that period can conceive what a spell there was in the uniform. What lofty expectations inflamed all the young heads on which a plume of feathers waved for the first time!

Every French soldier carries in his cartouch-box his truncheon of marshal of France; the only question is how to get it out. In this we found no difficulty whatever; nay, I think now that we had not then confined our dreams of ambition even to that limit.

One thing disturbed us:—If, said we, Napoleon should stop short in so glorious a career, if he should unfortunately take it into his head to make peace, farewell to all our hopes. Luckily, our fears were not realized, for he cut out more work for us than we were able to perform.

The Velites were soldiers in the imperial guard; the premium which they paid procured them the honour of serving their apprenticeship with the *élite* of the *élite* of the army. They arrived full of zeal; at first they thought that the exercise was not long enough, but they soon began to complain that it lasted too long: their novice's fervour abated. I recollect it well; I passed through all these different phases.

A fortnight after my arrival, I had been so assiduous that I was deemed worthy of mounting guard for the first time. When once installed at the post, the old chasseurs who were with me began to enumerate all the young Velites, who, in a similar situation to mine, had paid their footing by ordering a treat for their comrades from the neighbouring restaurateur. Such a one had done the thing handsomely, such another had been stingy, and barely given them as much as they could drink; while a third had behaved magnificently—pork-chops, bottled wines, coffee, spirits. I told them that I would do like this last. I was unanimously proclaimed a good fellow by the whole troop.

During the repast I was overwhelmed with praises. The aptitude which I showed in my first essays, and my extraordinary cleverness in the manual exercise, were highly extolled. Never, said the old grumblers, had any one mounted guard so soon: none of the Velites had attained that excess of honour till two months after their admission; all declared that I should get forward, that high destinies awaited me.

Though a novice, I was not silly enough to take literally all these encomiums that were lavished on the founder of the feast: I saw clearly that they were addressed to my entertainment. Still all this was gratifying to me. I had my flatterers—I, a private soldier; these flatterers were the conquerors of Egypt and of Italy; those old moustached foxes bepraised a lad whose virgin chin had never yet passed under the hand of the barber. After this, be surprised, if you please, that in the highest classes there are courtiers, and people who believe them on their word. Every one has in this world a little circle that flatters him: those who compose it move round him as the planets around the sun. Such persons, retiring to their own homes, become centre and sun in their turn. Thus the courtier, on leaving the sovereign, finds courtiers waiting for him; even these latter have others; and so on down to the very lowest of all.

On that day I scratched my name with my bayonet on the wall behind the sentry-box. Accident having lately carried me to the gate of the Champ de Mars, I thought I would see whether it was still legible; after a long search, I found it, covered with moss. The dinner at the corps de garde came into my memory with all its joyous circumstances. Is there one of the party left, besides myself? said I, thinking of all the events that had succeeded one another during an interval of thirty years. If any old chasseur had at that moment shown his face, tanned by the sun of the pyramids, how heartily I should have hugged him! Oh, the capital dinner that we made together!

In garrison, the soldiers of the imperial guard were little Sardanapaluses in comparison with those of the line. To each mess there was a female cook, a Sybarite luxury, for which the former were jeered, but at the same time envied, by the others.

Many of the Velites grew tired of the soldier's life, and, in order to become officers the sooner, transferred themselves to the military school of Fontainebleau. Others, after applying for admission into the school, and finding no vacancy, urged by impatience to put on the uniform as speedily as possible, entered the Velites, the elastic ranks of which always opened for a new-comer. I belonged to the latter class. When my turn came to go to Fontainebleau, I left the army: I had then to begin my education over again. In the Velites we were trained to the horse exercise; there we manœuvred on foot: I had to relinquish the carbine for the musket. In the imperial guard, the hair was worn cut into a brush before, and a queue behind: at the military school, the toupet was retained without the queue: so that, for six months cropped before, cropped behind, I was cropped everywhere, and my shorn head looked almost exactly like that of a singing boy.

General Bellavenne was governor of the military school of Fontainebleau. All who ever knew him will agree that the appointment seemed to have been created expressly for him. We thought him severe, but we thought wrong: when a man has six hundred heads of eighteen to govern, it is difficult to keep them in order without great severity. His *alter ergo*, the brave Kuhman, seconded him most admirably. That epithet *brave* was given to him by a man who was a consummate judge—by Napoleon himself. He was an excellent Alsatian, mangling the French language, whose hobby was discipline, and who thought of nothing but the exercise. I see him still at his door, at the moment when the battalion was getting under arms, stretching himself three inches taller, and crying:—" Heads up! heads up!—immovable!—immobility is the finest movement of the exercise!"

The antiquary exploring the Parthenon or the ruins of

Baalbeck, the painter contemplating the masterpieces of Raphael or Michael Angelo, the dilettante seated in the pit of the Italian Opera, the sportsman who sees his pointer make a dead set, feel less intense delight than did the brave Kuhman in seeing a platoon manœuvre according to principles. When a movement was well executed, when an evolution was effected in an accurate and precise manner, tears trickled from his eyes down his cheeks, blackened by gunpowder; he could not find words to express his gratification; he contemplated his work, and admired himself. "There is nothing finer," he would sometimes say, "than a soldier carrying arms. Immovable, head upright, chest forward—'tis superb! 'tis magnificent! 'tis touching!"

The drum awoke us at five in the morning. The courses of history, geography, mathematics, drawing, and fortification, occupied us from hour to hour; we recreated ourselves by change of study, and, to vary our pleasures, four hours of exercise skilfully distributed, diversified our day in a very agreeable manner; so that we lay down at night with our heads full of the heroes of Greece and Rome, rivers and mountains, angles and tangents, ditches and bastions. All these things were mixed up rather confusedly in our minds; the exercise alone was a positive matter: our shoulders, our knees, and our hands, prevented us from confounding that with the rest.

Novels were prohibited in the military school: one of our officers had a great horror of them. As he took his rounds through the halls of study, he confiscated without mercy everything that appeared to him to belong to the *Bibliothèque bleue*. He knew the titles of the books that we ought to have; all others were reputed to be novels, and deemed liable to seizure and condemnation as lawful prizes.

It was required that the pupils should have learned Latin; it was not taught at the school, and, of course, Virgil was not in our officer's catalogue. One evening, in the hall of study, I was reading the Eneid; he came behind me, and pounced upon my book like a vulture upon a nightingale.

"Another novel!" he exclaimed with an air of triumph.

"You are mistaken; it is Virgil."

"What does he treat of, this Virgil?"

"Of the siege of Troy, of wars, of battles . . . ."

"Troy! Troy! 'tis fabulous: I was right enough—another novel! Read the *Ecole de Peloton*—that is the best book for forming youth. If you must have amusement, imitate your neighbour. He instructs himself at the same time; he is a young man who spends his time to good purpose; if he lays aside that most interesting of all books, the Regulations of 1791, it is philosophical works that he takes up: he does not waste his time like you upon mawkish fictions." My neighbour, be it known, was reading *Thérèse Philosophe*.

"Only see how perverse these pupils are! In order to baffle me, they get novels printed in ciphers!" Such was the exclamation of our worthy officer when confiscating the Tables of Logarithms.

Our fare at the school resembled that of the soldiers in barracks; ammunition-bread, soup, and French beans in turn with other pulse: it was the strictly necessary without superfluity, as you may perceive. The introduction of every sort of dainty was prohibited. Now, young people are fond of dainties, and our invention was continually on the rack to devise new methods of smuggling. The porter, a stern custom-house officer, seized everything that looked at all like contraband; not for the purpose of re-exportation, but for his own benefit, and God knows whether he kept strict watch or not.

We went once a week into the forest of Fontainebleau, either to take plans or to work the guns. The officers of artillery and the professors of mathematics, who were with us on that day, much more indulgent than the officers who superintended the police of the school, permitted us to visit a crowd of itinerant cooks, piemen, and confectioners, who surrounded us with baskets full of very good things, the privation of which gave us a higher relish for them. There was a sort of tacit understanding that the officers were not to notice what was passing for a quarter of an hour. And what was the consequence? The youths ate much and hastily; several of them returned to the school with overloaded stomachs and indigestions, which next day rendered it necessary to send them to the infirmary. Every week the same thing produced the same effects, which made the doctor remark that the canons of the school were not less dangerous to us than the cannon of the enemy.

Like the Parisians, who go to enjoy themselves beyond the barriers, we could not introduce anything fradulently but in our stomachs. On our return we were always examined by piercing eyes, sometimes searched by expert hands, and smugglers were sure to be punished. Still it was disagreeable, after having had as much fowl, ham, pastry, as you liked for one day, to return on the next to a dish of lentils without sauce. The difference was too enormous; to soften it down by insensible demi-tints, and to prolong our gastronomic enjoyments, I invented cartouch-box pasties. This sublime invention gained me the most flattering encomiums from my comrades, and enrolled my name among those of the benefactors of the school.

You know, courteous reader, or perhaps you don't, how a cartouch-box is constructed: it is a leather box, containing a piece of wood perforated with holes to receive the cartridges. When we went out on the weekly expeditions to which I have been adverting, we had our muskets and our cartouch-boxes, but they were empty. One day, when, in the forest of Fontainebleau, I was conversing with due gravity on a matter of business with a vender of pastry, a luminous idea darted across my brain: the most ordinary person sometimes has his flashes of genius. I took out the piece of wood, of which I have been speaking; I gave it to the mar-sauce, and told him to make for us a number of pasties, of precisely that form. I acquainted all my comrades with the circumstance. A week afterwards, each of us, before we set off, left the perforated piece of wood under his bed, and we returned by beat of drum, with a smuggled pasty, which we had the pleasure to secrete from the vigilance of all the custom-house officers of the school. We pursued the same course every week. While I remained at Fontainebleau the secret was strictly kept; but, as everything, not excepting even the most useful, has an end in this best of all possible worlds, the cartouch-box pasties must have had their unlucky day.

General Bellavenne gave one day a grand dinner to the officers of the school and to the principal people of Fontainebleau. Thirty persons, invited to it, were in his drawing-room. The pupils, walking before the kitchen-windows, smelt a mass of combined odours, which produced the highest degree of irritation in the salivary glands of the mouth and the mucous membrane of the stomach. Reasoning by analogy, and comparing their recollections, they deduced from them the inference that the general's dinner must be an excellent one. Some intrepid fellows, scorning to eat their dry bread to this scent, resolved immediately to try the talents of the cook by a more positive test than that of smell.

Like grenadiers taking a redoubt by assault, they stormed the kitchen: cook and scullions were seized and thrust into sacks, head foremost. Into another sack they put woodcocks and partridges, salmon and turbot, hot and cold pasties, turkey stuffed with truffles. All these things formed a singular medley: no matter; the invaders did not stand upon trifles: they carried off, distributed, and devoured the whole. The general and his officers arrived, glowing with anger, like men who have lost their dinner. They sought, searched, turned over and over again, questioned, but found nothing, learned nothing. They ordered us all to our rooms, but this did not prevent them from making a sorry dinner, and they never knew who were the authors of their disappointment.

The supreme *bon ton* of the School was to smoke; in the first place, because it was forbidden, and in the next, because it was thought to give one a military air. Tobacco was smuggled in, night and day, in small quantities; but ever so small a stream that is constantly running will at length fill the basin. From morning till night the drummers were engaged in no other business, and yet they could scarce supply the demands of the consumers.

It would seem that with many people smoking is a thing of the first necessity, like bread, like air. One day, when several officers were conversing before me of the privations of all sorts which they had suffered, before, during, and after the battle of Eylau—one complained that he had not tasted bread for three days, another that he had been obliged to eat horseflesh, a third that he had nothing whatever to eat, while an old officer of hussars exclaimed, with the utmost gravity: "But only think of me—for five days together I had nothing to smoke but hay!"

Duels were frequent at the military school. Before my arrival, it was customary to fight with the bayonet; but, one of the pupils having been killed, the use of that weapon was forbidden. This prohibition did not suppress the practice: they would procure pieces of foils, and, in case of need, tie a pair of compasses to the end of a stick; and all to gain the reputation of hair-brained fellows. When any one had, by a duel, acquired this character, and could add to it that of a smoker, he had attained the pinnacle of glory.

One fine day, at a review, General Bellavenne proclaimed the names of those who were to set out on the morrow for the army. Oh! what emotions while he was reading the list! our hearts throbbed as if they would have burst our sides. What joy among the elect! what anxiety among those whose names had not yet been called over! To don an officer's frock, to wear the epaulet, to gird on a sword— Oh, what gratification at eighteen! We were soldiers; a moment afterwards we became officers: a word had produced this happy metamorphosis. Man is a child in all his life; at all ages he has his toys; he frequently esteems himself according to the dress that he wears: he is perhaps in the right, because the multitude judges by that standard. Be this as it may, with our sub-lieutenant's epaulets, we thought something of ourselves.

A captain of the school was commissioned to take us to the Emperor's head-quarters. We travelled post, so it was said; the truth is, that we were crowded by dozens into carts, and that it took us a whole day, from morning till night, to proceed two stages. Before our departure we had written to the principal restaurateur at Montereau, to prepare, against our arrival there a dinner for one hundred and twenty-seven, at twenty francs per head; but as soon as the column of carts had left the school, it was surrounded by all the venders of eatables. It was for us that for three days all the spits had been turning, all the ovens baking, all the cooks cooking. The town of Fontainebleau must have felt the removal of the school to St. Cyr: we were terrible consumers.

If it is disagreeable to be endowed with a ravenous appetite without being able to satisfy it with good things, it is also extremely unpleasant when you come to a table sumptuously spread and find it physically impossible to swallow a morsel. Such was precisely the state of us all, on our arrival at Montereau. What was to be done? Incapable of acting, we were obliged to confine ourselves to the sad part of spectators. After sincerely deploring our improvidence, and paying our reckoning, we sent for all the poor and all the blackguards of the town, and gave ourselves the treat of seeing them officiate in our stead.

The ambition of all of us was to assume a certain air of profligacy: we smoked, we drank drams, conceiving that these commendable habits would give us a military appearance. Our uniform, our swords, our epaulets were all new, all fresh from the shops. We exposed them to the rain and sun, that they might impart to them somewhat of the look of the bivouac. The school buttons and our beardless chins nevertheless betrayed us; and Captain Dornier, who marched at our head, plainly showed that, with our epaulets of a week old, we were yet but schoolboys.

We travelled gaily on, for we were young, without care, and full of hope. In traversing Prussia, then Poland, and then Prussia again, faring sometimes well, at others ill, we were constantly laughing. It was at Thorn, the birthplace of Copernicus, that we began to perceive the proximity of the grand army. That town, encumbered with depôts of almost all the regiments, had half of its houses transformed into hospitals. We were obliged to put up with lodgings in garrets and stables; there was nothing to be had between the two. We began to be sensible that, after all, war might not be the most agreeable thing in the world.

The army then occupied the cantonments which it took after the battle of Eylau, gained by the French, and by the Russians, as they assert. Napoleon was at Finkenstein, reviewing troops, repairing the losses of the month of February, communicating to all his extraordinary activity. There, I beheld, for the first time, that surprising man, of whom some would fain make a god, while certain idiots insist that he was but a fool. He has proved that he was neither the one nor the other. The opinions expressed concerning him have hitherto been too near the events to be exempt from partiality. No good history of Napoleon can be written for a long time to come: it is requisite for this purpose that contemporaries and their children should have passed away, that enthusiasm should have cooled, that animosities should be extinguished. Then, and not till then, a man free from passions, consulting the thousands of volumes written, and that are yet to be written, will be able to find truth in the well. With these materials will be raised a superb, an imperishable, monument. I bring my mite in aid of this grand work.

We manœuvred before the Emperor, who appeared well satisfied, and next day we were dispersed among all the regiments of the army.

At the head-quarters of Finkenstein I rejoined my comrades of the Velites, and had the satisfaction to see that my epaulets were an object of envy to them all. I began to get used to them, and the congratulations which I received, restored to them all the charms of novelty. Many things are of value in the estimation of men, solely from the envy which they excite in those who cannot possess them. Many a child takes up again a plaything, of which he had long grown weary, because a little friend comes in, and finds it extremely amusing.

EDITOR'S REMARKS

ON

CHAPTER I.

The concluding observations of the first chapter are trite. If thousands of volumes have been written upon the achievements of one man by his contemporaries, we may surely find truth without much trouble, for the well in which she lies ensconced cannot be very deep. Napoleon was the greatest man of modern times. His rivals among the ancients were Alexander the Great, Cæsar, and Hannibal. Like all other men, Napoleon was ambitious. He was not sanguinary. He was greatly beloved by the army and by the people of France. Being mortal, he committed errors; the attempt to seize Spain was, perhaps, his greatest misdeed; it was as criminal, though not so successful, or so cruel in its execution, as the conquest of India by England. But God is just. The French were deservedly beaten in Spain. The English rule totters in the East. Napoleon could not commit a small crime; his situation was so elevated, that the least deviation from rectitude had immense results; the slightest error in judgment was attended by great mischief; for the oak cannot fall like the acorn: he was, like all other sovereigns, exposed to temptation, and like them was tempted: the Saviour alone could stand upon the high mountain, and say:—" Get thee behind me, Satan!"

But, whether the crimes of Napoleon were few or many, it is admitted, even by his enemies, that his virtues were grand and numerous, and men proclaim him to have been the most powerful and the most extraordinary man that history records; Alexander was born a prince, and inherited a kingdom; Hannibal and Cæsar were also born princes in their respective oligarchies; Napoleon was self-exalted. All these things are admitted. What, then, do we wait for? What are we to expect from posterity? That Napoleon was great, we know. That he had faults and virtues, we know. The only answer that I can discover to the above questions is, that posterity will have to recount the *details* of Napoleon's great actions. But can it do this better than we can, who are his contemporaries? Posterity has also another task; having made up its mind as to details, it is then to supply the emperor with motives! It appears to some that contemporaries have the advantage over posterity. Others maintain the contrary, and that we, who are alive, are prejudiced; and that our descendants, who are neither dead nor alive, are to be a superior race. The author of this volume, who is a clever and an agreeable writer, is among the latter, and, indeed, the opinion seems universal. It may, however, be worth while to examine into its value.

The author says that our posterity must write the life of Napoleon, and decide, I will not say whether he was a god or a fool, because, as M. Blaze justly remarks, the people who call him a fool are " idiots," but on the degree of merit in execution and motive to which Napoleon is entitled for each of his actions. His greatness having been a point settled by the present generation, our unborn historian is, therefore, to recount the details and the motives of the execution of the Duke D'Enghien, the invasion of Spain, the advance into Russia, and other matters. On all these points, we, who have the means, are said to be too prejudiced to decide. Let us judge from the experience which facts teach us. The best and most celebrated and most unprejudiced histories have been written by contemporary authors, such as Xenophon, Thucydides, Cæsar, Polybius, Tacitus, Davila: are these prejudiced authors? Then, with regard to those who write of by-gone days, is the philosophical Hume unprejudiced? Are there not many histories of times which are long past, that are full of prejudices? Do they not generally copy one from another? How few examine original works, and when they do so, what is this but to give a preference to contemporaneous historians? Does not all depend upon the mind of the author, and upon his industry in collecting good materials, not upon the time in which he writes? I am strongly tempted to refer to Colonel Napier's History of the Peninsular War, which I believe to be unprejudiced, not judging by my own partiality, but because I have seen it attacked with all the virulence of personal and party animosity, and yet pass through the ordeal unconfuted, and therefore unharmed in public opinion.

We know that posterity must be the judge of all contemporaneous history, but what hopes of correctness as to facts can be expected from future historians, who are to write the history of our own times? Must not all their facts be drawn from the men of the present day, whose opinions, and the documents upon which they have been formed, must abide the decision of unborn men. The business, then, of existing authors is to pride themselves on being accurate, and to attack prejudice and inaccuracy with a dauntless pen. Thousands will in future search their pages, and sift their every word, in order to quote them as authorities for their own books; these future writers may be prejudiced, but they will not have any personal animosity against the authors of past days, and they will judge them by the accuracy or inaccuracy of their statements. If, like some of the ancients, they can bear a rigid examination, no man will attempt, three hundred years hence, again to write the history of times and events that have been well told by an actor in the scenes which that actor describes.

Whether a future history of Napoleon will display less prejudice than one which some military man may write in these days, I much doubt. The character of Napoleon produces enthusiastic admirers now. It will do the same to the end of time. The biographer of Napoleon *now*, while facts are all fresh and vivid, must feel that his fame as an author depends on his impartiality; and this impression will be more powerful in proportion as his abilities are commanding. We confound the duties of the present generation, who are witnesses, with those of the future generation, who form the jury; and we expect that the latter will depose to the facts, while they are called upon only to pass a verdict. The world will, in all ages, recur to the depositions of the witnesses to the facts, and it is the business of existing authors to furnish them. No man will prefer Livy to Polybius for an accurate statement of facts connected with the Carthaginian wars; indeed, Livy himself, by committing plagiary upon the work of the Grecian author, seems to have tacitly confessed the superiority of the latter, in his account of the second Punic war. The battle of Zama was fought two hundred years B.C., and Polybius was born two hundred and six years B.C., so that he was five years of age when Zama was fought, and about thirty-eight when brought prisoner to Rome, where he became the friend of Scipio, the grandchild by adoption of Scipio Africanus; and with this Scipio (Æmilianus), surnamed Africanus the younger, he fought when Carthage was destroyed, fifty-one years after the battle of Zama. Now, as Polybius came to Rome about sixteen years after the last-named battle, the whole story must have been fresh—indeed, scarcely told; for we have seen twenty-four years pass since the battle of Waterloo was fought, and the "model of Waterloo" has but just appeared, while fresh incidents of this great engagement daily come to light: all is yet vivid in men's eyes! Just so was the freshness of Zama in the days of Polybius, and the story of Hannibal is told by the friend of Scipio. Yet no posterior historian has accused the contemporary of partiality, or attempted to give a better history.

Prejudices very rarely enter into the works of a great historian; though he must bear from his own generation the accusation of being prejudiced. Each nation, each faction, each family, nay, each vain-glorious individual, takes up arms against him, if particular partialities be not fed by unqualified praise. These partialities form the rule of *impartiality* with men of an ordinary stamp. But the historian, whose firm and capacious mind is above such weakness, pursues his course unshaken by their puny assaults, and writes for future applause. Such a contemporary can write the life of Napoleon. If such a man does not arise, posterity may justly reproach the literature of the present age, as being so feeble that it could not grapple with this glorious subject.

As to the pretended life of Napoleon by Sir Walter Scott, it may be easily set aside. Every one must admire Sir Walter

Scott as a romance-writer: he has delighted society; but when he pretends to write history, the case is quite changed. I will not enter upon a criticism of his life of Napoleon, but merely ask whether the life of a warrior can be written by a man totally ignorant of war? If a shoemaker were to attempt to write the life of a great surgeon, he might, perhaps, give a tolerable account of the gossip held in the patients' rooms by the servants; but he assuredly would give but a lame account of surgical operations. He would tell us that the doctor killed this man and saved that, but he could not tell why; all would be mere assertion, or a hearsay theory of ignorant old women, or of enemies; he could not form any judgment of his own, nor tell what was the result of certain medicines, or certain operations, nor could he form any correct judgment of the symptoms which rendered such practice proper or improper. In short, he would state that his hero was born, lived and died, where he went to school, where and with what success he practised; but his professional merits, the character of the diseases which he treated and the causes of success would be far beyond the shoemaker's power, and the old proverb would be realized, that the " shoemaker should not go beyond his last." Just so with the life of Napoleon by Sir Walter Scott, and all the lives of military men which are written by non-military authors.

I speak of them quite independently of their political partialities or their impartialities; I refer merely to their professional callings; and common sense tells us that, to do justice to the histories of wars and of warriors, they must be written by military men.

But, because Walter Scott and others have failed in their lives of Napoleon, there is no reason to suppose that some young historian may not yet arise who will succeed; some young and eloquent soldier, with a genius able to comprehend the great character of the emperor, and to do him justice.

This I hope and believe will be the case, and I cannot allow that being contemporaneous with transactions is an insuperable objection to their being justly and eloquently recorded.

CHAPTER II.

THE BIVOUAC AND MARAUDERS.

HERE we are, then, in a charming plain, cut up by the artillery, trampled by the cavalry. It has rained the whole day. It is here that we are to sleep. The order is given: twenty men of each company are sent to the neighbouring villages to fetch wood, straw, and provisions. A curious sight soon presents itself to our view. "The fair will be a good one," say the soldiers, "the dealers are coming." On all sides we see, in fact, our intrepid freebooters arriving laden with sacks of poultry, baskets of eggs, and files of loaves stuck upon the ramrods of their pieces. Some are driving before them sheep and cows, oxen and pigs: others are making peasants, whom they have put in requisition, carry straw and wood for them. From the sour looks of the latter, and from the interjections that escape them, you plainly perceive that they are far from pleased; but their words are drowned by the cries of the animals and by the loud laughter of the soldiers.

Meanwhile, fires are kindled, the pots begin to boil, night comes on, each has made his little arrangements for sheltering himself: but an aide-de-camp, a real mar-feast, comes at full gallop; and presently an order, transmitted from left to right, puts an end to our plans, and suspends our preparations. We must decamp without drum or trumpet: we are to sleep a few thousand paces farther. The fires are to be left alight on the spot that we are quitting, we are to kindle others elsewhere, to make the enemy believe that we have twenty thousand men there, while in reality there are but ten thousand. This manœuvre is, no doubt, very scientific, but it is not the most agreeable to the ten thousand men.

All at once the pots are lifted off; the meat, just beginning to boil, is taken out of them smoking, wrapped in a wisp of straw, and tied to the knapsacks: and we start to begin again precisely what we have just been doing. Fresh fires are lighted, and presently there is nothing of them to be seen.

When the army is in bivouac, in presence of the enemy, every man lies down in his clothes, sleeping, as it were, with eyes open: it is necessary to be ready for whatever may happen. Sometimes we have been a month without pulling off our boots; a trial which, in the end, becomes extremely painful. Sometimes, too, when we had lain down, we took a fancy to unbutton the coat, and then the trousers; we slackened one buckle, and then another; and afterwards it took more time to set matters to rights than if we had completely undressed ourselves. When the weather is cold, everybody lies down near the fire; but you roast on one side, while you freeze on the other; you certainly have the resource of turning, like St. Lawrence, but it is not at all convenient.

When you are in second line, you may then undress, as less precaution need then be observed. The officers have linen bags, into which they creep, and which serve them for sheets. As the mattress and feather-bed are always replaced by two trusses of straw, the cloth sack is much more agreeable than sheets, because it does not suffer anything to penetrate into the inside.

The moment for rousing at the bivouac is never amusing. You have slept because you were fatigued; but when you rise, your limbs feel stiff; your moustaches like tufts of clover, are impearled, every hair of them, with dew-drops; the teeth are clenched, and you must rub the gums for a considerable time to restore the circulation. These little inconveniences are continually happening, even when the weather is fine, but, when it is rainy or cold, the situation is a great deal worse, and hence it is that heroes have the gout and the rheumatism.

Those who have never been engaged in war cannot form any idea of the calamities that it brings in its train. I shall not give a complete description of them; that would exceed the bounds which I have prescribed for myself. I shall merely say a few words concerning our life at the bivouac, and the waste made by the army. We lived upon what the soldiers *found*—a soldier never steals anything, he only finds it—and it was not possible to do otherwise: our rapid marches prevented our magazines from following us, when we had magazines. In rich countries, twenty times the quantity of provisions that it was possible to consume was brought to the camp; the rest was wasted. The soldier lives from hand to mouth: yesterday he was destitute of everything; to-day he is in abundance; he forgets the privations of yesterday, and gives himself no concern about the morrow: neither does it occur to him that in the following days other regiments will arrive at the position which he is about quitting, and that, while taking for himself what is necessary, it would be well to leave something for those who are to come after him. Such an idea never enters his head. A company of one hundred men has already killed two oxen —these are sufficient: they have besides *found* four cows, six calves, twelve sheep; they are all slaughtered without mercy, that they may regale themselves with the tongues, the kidneys, the brains. They enter a cellar where twenty pipes present an imposing and majestic battle-array; they have no tools for boring holes, but soldiers are never at a loss: they fire with ball at the staves, and presently twenty fountains of wines are playing on all sides, amid bursts of laughter from the actors. If one hundred pipes were in the cellar, they would all be broached at once, for they have a right to try which is the best. All runs away, all is wasted, and it very often happens that the tipplers drink to such excess that they fall down and are drowned in the flood of wine which inundates the cellar.

Austria is a country fertile in all things: at each bivouac we left enough to subsist a regiment for a fortnight. The soldiers, after marching all day, spent great part of the night in seeking provisions, cooking and eating them. They indulged as little as possible in sleep; the whole time for rest they spent in making fricassees, pancakes, and fritters. As their stomachs were not strong enough to endure this incessant eating and drinking, the consequences were numerous indigestions, which filled the hospitals with sick. To an army, abundance is sometimes more injurious than want.

The supreme happiness with soldiers consists in gormandizing. In general, they would rather cook and coddle for themselves, than have two good meals supplied them at regular hours. In the environs of Ling, I was quartered with all my company on a wealthy farmer. Our host begged me to maintain discipline in his farm-yard, promising to furnish my men with everything necessary. They lay upon straw in a very spacious barn, and were supplied with three abundant and well-dressed meals a day. In going my rounds, I took it into my head to ask my fellows if they were satisfied with the way in which they were treated.

" Why, as for that matter," said they, " not exactly."

" I understand that your meals are good and abundant; it is right that, after so many fatigues, you should have some compensation."

" We have not a great deal to complain of . . . . but . . . ."

" Is what they give you to eat bad ?"

" No, . . . but . . . "

" Is not the quantity sufficient ?"

" Yes, . . . but . . . "

"But . . . but . . . but . . . why don't you speak out? What had you yesterday for dinner?"

"Soup, bouilli, a dish of vegetables, roast mutton, a salad, cheese, a bottle of wine per man, and a small glass of brandy."

"The devil! and you are not content!"

"Pardon me, lieutenant, but . . ."

"I wish you may never fare worse."

"Ah! *pardi!*" said an old corporal, stepping up to me, "it is very good of you to take the trouble to convince those chaps that they are well off; but give them roasted angels, and they would still grumble."

They would, no doubt, have been much better pleased to have had less, and to prepare their meals themselves. They were enraged to see the oxen, the sheep, the poultry, and the pigeons, quiet in the farm-yard, and reposing on the faith of treaties. They would have liked to fall upon them with musket and sabre, to slaughter them all, to fritter all away in a single day, and then to proceed in the same manner in the neighbouring villages.

Another motive urges some of the soldiers to undertake the duty of procuring necessaries: while professedly searching for provisions, they enter houses, and sometimes find means to possess themselves of the purses of the owners. To search for provisions is an excellent pretext; when they do not receive regular allowances, it is impossible to prevent them from pillaging. The grand excuse of the marauders of an army is this:—"I am hungry; I am searching for bread." This declaration admits of no reply. When you have not bread to give them, you must let them procure it how and where they can. The cavalry have a double excuse: they are seeking forage for their horses. A cuirassier was surprised by his captain while rummaging a chest of drawers.

"What are you about there?" said the officer angrily.

"Seeking some oats for my horse."

"A likely place to look for oats!"

"I have just found in the peasant's library a bundle of hay, between a thousand leaves of paper; why may I not meet with oats in this chest of drawers?"

The brave cuirassier had robbed the botanist of his herbarium, without discovering in it anything but an armful of hay for his horse.

It may not be amiss to remark here that the soldiers give the appellation of peasants to all who are not military men. My Philistine—so we call the soldiers who officiate for us as servants—said to me, one day: "A peasant is come to invite you to take soup (to dine) with him to-morrow, lieutenant."—"What is his name?"—"Why, it is the baron, at whose house you lodged last week."

In every regiment, in every company, there were determined plunderers, who marched on the outskirts of the track, two or three leagues from the column. Sometimes they were attacked by the enemy; but I can assert with truth, that the intelligence of the French soldier is equal to his bravery. These fellows chose one of their number for their chief, who commanded them as absolute dictator; and these new-made generals have fought serious battles, and gained victories.

During the retreat of the British army under Sir John Moore, to Corunna, our advanced guard which pursued it arrived, to its great astonishment, at a village surrounded by a palisade. The tricoloured flag waved on the steeple; the sentinels wore the French uniform. Some officers went up to it, and they soon learned that for three months past two hundred marauders had occupied that village. Their retreat being cut off, they had established themselves in this post, which they had fortified. Though frequently attacked, they had always repulsed the enemy. Their commander-in-chief was a corporal; sovereign of this colony, his orders were obeyed as implicitly as those of the Emperor. The officers, on entering the village, proceeded to the residence of the commandant: he was out shooting with his staff. In a short time he returned and related his story, which showed how much bravery, seconded by intelligence, is capable of accomplishing.

This corporal, with his experience acquired by long habit, had fortified this village as well as any officer of engineers could have done; and, what is remarkable, he had contrived to conciliate in the highest degree the good-will of the inhabitants. At his departure he received from the alcalde the most honourable testimonials; we have known many generals who could not produce such.

From time to time, distributions of provisions were made to the army; pillage was then strictly forbidden, and terrible examples were frequently made; but this system was not followed up, and was enforced only by fits and starts.

When we were staying for a few days in or near a town, the principal concern of all these marauders was to get rid of the money which they had *found* in their nocturnal excursions. They dreaded but one thing, that was to die with a full purse. If they obtained leave for one day, they would take three. An hour before the expiration of the third day, they arrived at the bivouac where their regiment was, for they well knew that after that time they would be set down as deserters. At Vienna, at Berlin, at Warsaw, they were seen returning in elegant carriages which they had hired, accompanied by ladies, whose affection was in a direct ratio to the dollars that were still left in the pockets of these Lotharios, from whom they would not part but in the last extremity.

Knowing beforehand the punishment that awaited them, they ordered the drivers to take them to the camp guardhouse, which serves for a prison when in the field. Thither the carriages accordingly proceeded, amidst the shouts, the applauses, of their envious comrades. As soon as they were installed, they sent word to the captain and the sergeant-major; and during their confinement they amused themselves with relating minutely the games at billiards they had played, and sumptuous feasts they had enjoyed, the bottles they had drunk, and the like.

"Lieutenant," said Dieudonné, the most intrepid marauder of the army, to me, one day, "if you would give me permission, I would go to a village, which must be on the other side of this wood, for I hear the cocks crowing, and, probably, I should find some hens, too, there."

"You well know that it is forbidden."

"Yes, but if you would . . . ."

"What?"

"Only just not take notice that I am absent at the rappel."

"Get you gone, and contrive so that I know nothing about the matter."

Dieudonné returned with a cart laden with provisions, of which he made presents to the officers, to keep himself in favour; and, thanks to his activity, our table at the bivouac was always well supplied. Observe, too, that as we went along during the day, a few hares and a few partridges had swelled out our game-bag. When evening came, all these savoury materials were placed in the hands of a cook, who had formerly been an assistant at the Frères Provençaux, and whom the conscription had dragged from their famous kitchen; the smell was wafted far away, even to the enemy's videttes, and, when you recollect that we had been marching all day, you will easily conceive that we enjoyed our dinner. A good dinner is always a good thing; but, in war, as after hunting, no superlative is too strong to apply to it.

I shall perhaps be told, that it was wrong to authorize pillage: to this I reply, that my conscience has never reproached me on account of the pigeons, the pullets, the ducks, which I procured in this manner. We should have been stupid, indeed, if, while we were serving our generals as instruments for enriching themselves, we had not dared to indulge ourselves with a roasted chicken when their excellencies were pleased to forbid it. Very often they were well paid for these prohibitions; sometimes, too, they wished to gain at our expense a reputation for integrity, which some of them had great need of. They were like two ladies belonging to the court, who, by way of doing penance for the indulgences of the carnival, and finding all other ways too annoying for them, resolved to make their servants fast during Lent.

When a detachment of conscripts arrived, the first question put to each of them was what business he had followed before he had entered the service: when the young man owned the glorious title of cook, it became a point of dispute who should have him in his company. A cook!—he was an important personage at the bivouac: it is, in fact, nothing to possess the raw material; you ought to know, too, how to work it. A skilful artist subjects it to a thousand transformations: between a pullet cooked at a pot-house, and one set before the customers of the Rocher de Cancale, there is as wide a difference as between the moon and the sun.

These conscript cooks did not fight; they were left in the rear; we would not expose their precious lives. A captain falls; his lieutenant takes his place: but tell me, if you please, how you would replace a cook. In all ages, the duties of a cook have been highly appreciated by sovereigns and by the great. Henry VIII., who did not always jest, raised his cook to one of the highest dignities in England, for the skill which he had displayed in roasting a wild boar. The Emperor Wenceslaus ordered a scullion to be spitted and roasted, because he had suffered a sucking pig to stand and get scorched. Here were two sovereigns who knew how to punish and reward in a suitable manner!

Every captain had a man like Dieudonné; each of these

robbers was the chief of three or four others, who marched with him. To carry on this kind of profession, it was necessary to be indefatigable; for, after marching the whole day with the regiment, the marauders ran about all night; coming back in the morning to the camp, they started again with us, and scarcely ever lay down to rest themselves.

"Lieutenant," said one of these fellows to me, "I have got some famous wine, wine in case, and I have put aside some bottles for the officers of the company. We have tasted it, and I do assure you it is the best that ever was drunk: in short, you must know, it is *Posa piano.*" He had taken the direction given on the case for the name of the place which produced this wine. As far as I can recollect, the *Posa piano* was pronounced delicious by a jury of taste.

Some days before the battle of Friedland, we were assembled to the number of nearly fifty thousand in the plain of Guttstadt. Each man had made his preparations for passing the night with as little discomfort as possible, when reports of musketry proceeded from a small neighbouring wood. At the same time cries of *To arms!* were raised. We concluded that we were attacked by the enemy. All the pots were instantly emptied; the meat, which had been boiling for two hours, was slung to the knapsacks; the regiments formed in order of battle; and in an instant every man was at his post.

We expected to see some Russian column debouch, but the Russians had something else to do. They were dining, and we had made it impossible for ourselves to do the same. An enormous bull, which had escaped from the butchers, caused all this confusion; the enraged animal upset everything in his way. He overthrew whole platoons, which endeavoured to stop him with crossed bayonets: at length, however, he fell, pierced with balls. The soldiers began to make their soup again; but their meat, already boiled, had lost nearly all its juice, and yielded but a very weak broth. For a long time afterwards, the soldiers, when their soup was bad, would compare it with that of Guttstadt.

This circumstance occurred near the field of battle of Eylau, over which we passed on the following day; each recognized the position which he had occupied four months before, and also that of the enemy. Like the Trojans, after the retreat of the Greeks, our soldiers were delighted to revisit the spots which had witnessed their exploits and their dangers. For this famous battle *Te Deums* were sung in Paris and in Petersburg.

Pantagruel heard the shouts of combatants, and the cries of the wounded on a field of battle where not a creature was to be seen; and Pantagruel was, of course, very much astonished. Panurge then explained the mystery. These cries had been uttered in winter, and, as the cold was intense, they were frozen in the air; the sun thawing them by degrees, it was but natural to hear voices without seeing the speakers. If such a thing had happened on the day of the battle of Eylau, if the reports of the artillery and musketry had been frozen, what an uproar we should have heard on that day!

One fine night, we were in bivouac; I was not sleepy. Seated near the fire, I was smoking my pipe beside the soldier who was cooking the soup. Looking at the pot, which was boiling vehemently on the fire, I saw something black rising to the top, and sinking again to the bottom of the enormous kettle. This something excited my curiosity the more, inasmuch as, appearing at very short intervals, I had reason to imagine that it had two or three companions. Gallantly drawing my sword, and making a lunge at it as it passed, after missing it several times, I at length caught it on the point. In this way I fished out one mouse, two mice, three mice, four mice. I awoke our cook.

"Halloo, comrade! you seem to have got some strange seasoning for your soup to-night."

"The same as usual, lieutenant; potatoes and cabbage; I never put in anything else."

"And the whole boiled in mouse-broth. Only look at the nice vegetables that I have taken out of your pot."

"Impossible, lieutenant!"

"Possible enough and true enough. Where the devil did you get your water?"

"From a tub in the next village."

"Did you look if anything was in it?"

"It was dark; I felt that it was water, and took some for my soup. Who could suppose that in a peasant's tub there would be a squadron of mice?"

"You must throw away the soup and try to make more."

"Impossible, lieutenant: I should not have time. All those fellows that are snoring round us will awake presently; their stomachs will be open before their eyes; and if the soup should not be ready, they would be sure to give me fifty slaps, you know where. Let me beg of you, lieutenant, as the mice are out, not to say a word about them to anybody; the soup will be none the worse, and you may get out of the mess by breakfasting with another company."

"And you?"

"I shall take some of it, all the same."

And he did partake of it, and afterwards told me that he never tasted better soup in his life.

This circumstance is to be thus accounted for. At many farm-houses in Germany, in order to destroy the mice, they use a tub half-full of water. Some thin pieces of wood are placed at top, and upon them is put bacon, flour, or some other bait. As soon as the mice are upon this bridge, it sinks under them, they drop into the water, and are drowned. The piece of wood is so contrived as to resume its first position, and is ever ready to do its office. It was from a reservoir of this kind that our cook of the bivouac had taken the water of which he made his strange broth. However, the men, who knew nothing of the matter, thought it excellent.

Between the camp and the bivouac, properly so called, there exists something which is neither bivouac nor camp. In bivouac you are exposed, without shelter, to all weather; in camp, you live in regular barracks; but, in this something akin to both, you are under small sheds which screen you from the rain.

These are only constructed in places where you expect to stay for some days; for a single night one would not take so much trouble. These sheds consist merely of a straw roof upon three walls of straw. The open side is the highest, and the closed end is to windward. Each arranges for himself in the best manner he can, chooses what spot he likes, and the whole presents a very pretty picture.

In this sort of hut you cannot stand upright, except just at the entrance. You may sleep very well in them, but in the morning you have to make your toilet in the open air, which saves you the trouble of throwing up windows. What varied scenes a painter might find to sketch in such an encampment! but they would not all be admitted into the exhibition at the Louvre.

On the day of our arrival at Tilsit, there was talk of an armistice: sheds were immediately constructed of sufficient solidity to withstand the buffetting of the weather for a week. I had lain down one evening beside Laborie, my lieutenant, when we were visited by Hémeré, sub-lieutenant in our regiment. I was just falling asleep; his coming roused me again; but, from the turn which the conversation took, I thought fit to pretend not to be awake. The dialogue, which I shall never forget, was, word for word, as follows—

"Good evening, Laborie."

" Good evening; why, how is it that you are not a-bed ?"

" A-bed, indeed! I have something else to do, faith! I shall have to run about all night."

" It is said that we are going to have peace, that they have even signed an *amnesty;* and I believe it, for the quarter-master and the musicians have arrived."*

" Whether they make peace or war, I only know this, that, after marching all day, I shall have a fine night's work of it."

" What is the matter, then ?"

" The colonel has ordered me to seek a mill, which is six leagues off. I have nobody to direct me what way to take; the villages are forsaken, and there is not a peasant to serve me for a guide. All I can learn is, that the mill is called Brünsmühl. I have four cart-loads of corn to get ground; I am to take bakers along with me to make it into bread, which we are to bring back with us."

" Good news, my dear fellow! Make haste, and be sure, above all, to put aside two or three loaves for me."

" Of course I should do that, without bidding; but I am come to look at your map; I am told that you have one."

" Yes, I have one, and a capital one too."

" Do you think we shall find the mill ?"

" Find it! *pardi*, everything is in my map."

Now, you must know, that Laborie's map was a map of the world, which he had picked up at the bivouac among the various things *found* by the soldiers in marauding. To give himself an air of importance, Laborie would every moment spread out his map: we frequently concerted together, and, as fast as he folded it up, one of us would come in and make him spread it out again.

* The quarter-master, the musicians, and the master-tailor, follow their regiments at a distance, only when in the field. Whenever they join them, the soldiers cry: " Peace is made; here are the musicians."

"There is my map," said he, spreading it on the ground, and lying down at full length before it: "what is the name of your mill?"

"Brünsmühl."

"Let us see . . . . . stay . . . . . there is Berlin, there is Petersburg: it must be between the two."

"Quite right. . . .just so; yet I don't see the mill; perhaps it has been forgotten."

"Forgotten! everything is in my map, I tell you."

"And I tell you, that I can't see it."

"Why, there it is, though, and big enough too," said Laborie, pointing to the compass, placed in the margin, the four points of which were not unlike the sails of a windmill.

"So it is, I declare; the very thing!" exclaimed Hémeré, in admiration of Laborie's superior knowledge. "Do you think it is far off?"

"Why, no, see yourself." And Laborie measured with his hand the distance of the mill from the point midway between Berlin and Petersburg, which was not more than a foot.

"But what road must I take to get there?"

"It must be confessed that you are a very stupid fellow; the least thing embarrasses you; there's your road . . . only look at the map . . . . and there's the mill. Well, when you are out of this, you make for the right flank; keep straight on, and if you march quick, you'll soon be there."

My conscience began to reproach me for suffering this poor devil to run about all night in quest of the compass, and I was on the point of awaking; but M. Hémeré was a quarrelsome blade, rather foul-tongued, clamouring against the young men who had become officers without having served, like him, in the army of Sambre and Meuse; and so I resolved to leave him to his fate, that I might rally him on his return. I assure you he was not spared when he came back, three days afterwards, with his cart-loads of corn, without being able to find his mill.

M. Hémeré was a droll fellow, five feet high at most. He was very fond of physical gratifications; nay, I verily believe that he died without suspecting that there can be any others. His greatest, I may say, his only, pleasure, was to drink while smoking; and, for the sake of variety—I use his own expression—he would smoke while drinking. Lamenting one day, before me, the privations which he endured in the field for want of wine, brandy, and tobacco, his imagination immediately called up some most agreeable recollections.

"Oh! how well we fared," said he, "in the environs of Anspach and Ellwangen, where we were cantoned for six months! We had as much wine as we could drink; the peasants furnished everything that we required."

"If you only want as much wine as you can drink to make you happy," said I, "you are easily satisfied."

"And what the devil would you have more?" he replied. "In the morning, after exercise, I drank my two bottles to breakfast, which laid me asleep immediately. After snoozing for two or three hours, I took a third bottle, which I swallowed in bed, and went to sleep again till dinner. In the evening, a little walk, hot wine at my return; I went to bed upon it, and began again the next day. Never did I enjoy myself so much as in the environs of Ellwangen.

The finest of all bivouacs, past, present, and to come, was that of the 4th of July, 1809. Never was there so great an assemblage of men on so small a speck of the globe. The whole French army had crossed the Danube on three triple bridges, and was in the isle of Lobau, drenched by rain, which fell in torrents for six successive hours. Two hundred thousand men bivouacked together in close columns, by regiments. We had each of us scarcely room sufficient to stir. There was still an arm of the river to cross. The cannon thundered all night; the bombs poured down to defend it; the next day's battle, and the victory that was to follow—all this presented a superb prospect, held forth magnificent hopes.

Never before had the grand army been so collected. Every one recognized a friend in the veteran band which had come from Spain or Italy. Not only did individuals express their joy, but whole regiments manifested intense delight on meeting with other regiments with which they had shared danger and glory at the bridge of Arcole, at the Pyramids, at Marengo, at Hohenlinden. This fraternity of perils had strengthened friendship in some, and given birth to it in others. The friendships contracted in the field of battle are lasting. Old comrades had parted on the banks of the Nile or the Guadalquivir; they met again with transport in an island of the Danube.

The counters of the suttlers were beset by all those brave fellows, who, glass in hand, congratulated themselves on finding one another again. Each recounted the exploits of his regiment since the period of separation, and the list was a long one. Each, satisfied with himself, proud of his neighbour, had not the least doubt of victory. Like the soldiers of Casimir, all of them could have said to Napoleon: "Be easy, rely upon us; if the sky falls we will prop it up on the points of our lances." A moment afterwards they shook hands and parted. For a great number this was an everlasting adieu, for that day was the eve of the battle of Wagram.

All the nations had deputies in the isle of Lobau; all the languages of Europe were spoken there. The Italians and the Poles, the Mamelukes and the Portuguese, the Spaniards and the Bavarians—all those bands were astonished to find themselves marching under the imperial eagle. There, too, were seen Saxons and Westphalians, troops of Baden and of Wurtemberg; in those days our friends, but friends no longer. There was running hither and thither, there was seeking without finding, there was talking without being understood. It was a swarm in motion, the tower of Babel, the valley of Jehosaphat, where as everybody knows, we are all to meet some day or other.

EDITOR'S REMARKS

ON

CHAPTER II.

The description given of a French bivouac, in the second chapter, is very entertaining: I conclude that the picture is a correct one. But it does not describe an English bivouac; our soldiers do plunder, they do drink horribly, they do commit the excesses of which the author accuses his countrymen: at the same time, I must say, that I never saw British officers connive at, much less encourage, such conduct, without exciting disgust among their comrades, and drawing punishment upon themselves. I do not mean to say that there may not occasionally be found one or two officers sufficiently infamous to pillage; but I assert that, knowing their fate, if discovered, they act, like all other thieves, by stealth; and I assert still farther, that no organized bands of pillagers existed, and were recognized, in each regiment, by the officers. I was not aware that such was the case with the French; but, from the enormous size of the imperial army, I can easily believe that the evils of loose discipline were necessarily gigantic; indeed, the proof of this may be found in the emperor's ordering movable columns for the sole purpose of police. I therefore would cast no stigma on the armies of France: I am only surprised that the officers, as M. Blaze affirms, should not only tolerate, but profit by, the atrocities of these men, for I have ever looked upon the French officers as men of the highest honour.

When armies of several hundred thousand men are assembled, they are sometimes driven by necessity into courses that they would otherwise abhor. Our armies have no such excuse; they are comparatively small. We authorize not pillage, which we strenuously endeavour to prevent and punish. If the author be correct in his statements, and I suppose that he is so, then the difference between the two armies is this, that both pillage, but that in the French army the practice is tolerated; in the English army it is not tolerated.

Perhaps the difference has not been produced by any moral superiority in the British army, but by circumstances. I must, however, say that, having once entered a captured town with a French army, the military were as regular and correct in their conduct as any British troops. I have no right to doubt the assertions of the author, himself a French officer and a gentleman of ability; but I am unwilling to think that such a laxity of principle should exist among men so distinguished for their courage.

CHAPTER III.

MARCHES.

WE marched to the right, to the left, forward, sometimes backward; in short, we were always marching: very often we knew not why. The bobbin that turns round to wind the thread does not ask the mechanist the reason of the movements which it is forced to make; it turns, that is all: we did exactly like the bobbin. This was not always amusing, but the habit contracted, the necessity for obeying, the example which each set and took, had all concurred to make us mere locomotive machines: they move, so did we. When we halted, the soldiers, in astonishment, asked one another the reason. "'Tis droll," said they; "the clock stands."

On the day after the first bivouac of a campaign, whoever had seen the enormous quantity of breeches, long gaiters, black and white, collars, and stockings, that strewed the plain where we had slept, would imagine that the enemy had surprised us during the night, and that we had run away in our shirts. Perhaps you may like to know why all those garments were left there, widowed and deserted.

Formerly, the soldier was furnished, gratis, with a pair of breeches, which he scarcely ever put on: he was obliged to pay for a pair of trousers, which he always wore. The contractors for linen and shoes, speculators having an eye to consumption, crammed the knapsacks with long gaiters, white and black, stockings and collars, black and white, all of them articles serviceable only to those who sold them. In garrison, the soldiers were obliged to keep all these things, upon pain of having to pay for others the next day. But, on taking the field, at the first bivouac, every one reduced his kit to the smallest possible dimensions, by ridding himself of all useless articles.

The colonels and captains laughed in their sleeve; they were certain that, as soon as peace was made, they should have to provide and sell new ones in their stead. In like manner the booksellers rejoice when they see the missionaries make bonfires of the works of Rousseau and Voltaire.

Any one going after the army at such a time with vehicles, finding a complete load at the first bivouac, might have returned next day with as many pair of breeches as there were men in the ranks. The military administration has made immense progress since the peace. At present, the soldier is supplied with cloth trousers, and that is an improvement; the breeches no longer exist. I never could account for it that, under Napoleon, when we were incessantly at war, the soldier should have been clad in that ignoble short garment, which, clipping the leg, prevented him from marching freely. Nay more, the knee, covered with a long gaiter, which buttoned over it, was again clasped by a fresh garter compressing the knee-band of the breeches. Underneath, drawers tied by strings, also contributed to cramp the legs. Thus, in fact, there were three thicknesses of stuff, two rows of buttons placed one over the other, and three ties destined to paralyse the efforts of the most sturdy walkers.

Now tell me, if a person wished to devise a most inconvenient method of clothing the soldier, could he have hit upon one more to the purpose? Such was the practice during all the wars of the Republic and the Empire. Hence you should have seen the grotesque figure cut by the young conscripts, with these breeches and gaiters, which, not being kept up by calves, fell down about their heels. For this dress, a man should be well *built*, well made; he ought to have legs furnished with fair protuberances; whereas, wide trousers are suitable for everybody. A man of twenty is not yet formed; nay, we were joined by conscripts who were under nineteen; this accoutrement gave them an absolutely silly look: on the contrary, it sat extremely well on the imperial guard, which never fought unless in full dress, but which fought very rarely.

That body was moreover composed of picked men, who could easily have carried a heavier knapsack. It always marched on the high-road, with the head-quarters; it monopolized all the attention of the administration, and it may be asserted that the line had no supplies till the imperial guard was served. Our conscripts bent under the weight of a knapsack, a musket, a cartouch-box; add to these fifty ball-cartridges, bread, meat, a kettle, or perhaps a hatchet,* and you may form some conception of the plight of those poor

* Each mess, composed of twenty or thirty men, has a can, a pot, a hatchet, which are carried in turn by the men of the squad.

fellows, especially in hot weather. The perspiration trickled from their brows; and, in general, after marching for three successive days, they were obliged to go into the hospital. Our marches were far more toilsome than those of the imperial guard; we had to travel along much worse roads; and I think I am warranted in asserting that fatigue killed more young conscripts than the cannon of the enemy.

In 1806, Napoleon had adopted the white coat for the infantry; all the conscripts that came from France were dressed in jean, which formed a very disagreeable contrast when they were intermixed with other soldiers in blue uniforms. It was a preposterous idea to give a white dress to troops destined to pass their lives in bivouac.* You should have seen how dirty all these young men were: in consequence, the moment the Emperor set eyes on them, a counter-order was issued, and the white dress was abolished. This circumstance did not prevent the authors of the restoration from repeating the experiment in 1815. They at least had an excuse; they purposed to do as had formerly been done. But how could the Emperor, who made us always sleep in the open air, ever think that he should have a fine army with soldiers dressed in white!

The imperial guard was magnificent, and rendered important services wherever it appeared. This ought not to excite surprise; it was recruited from the crack companies of our regiments. The strongest and bravest men, who had seen four years' service and two campaigns, were selected for it. What might not be expected from a body thus composed! it was the *élite* of the *élite*. The soldiers of the line called those of the guard the *immortals*, because they very rarely fought. They were reserved for great

---

* This determination of the Emperor's was a corollary to the Berlin decree. As we could not procure indigo, except from England, Napoleon, by adopting a white dress for the army, meant to deprive English commerce of one of its branches.

occasions, and this course was no doubt extremely judicious, for the arrival of the imperial guard on the field of battle almost always decided the question. Between the line and the guard there subsisted a jealousy, which was the cause of many quarrels. It is well known that in the guard each had the rank of the grade immediately superior to that which he occupied. In the line loud complaints were raised against this privilege, and every one did his best to acquire it. Those who had obtained it deemed it perfectly just; they could not conceive how humble officers of the line could have the presumption to think of setting themselves on an equality with those of the imperial guard. Such is man, and such he will remain till the consummation of ages. In France, when everybody talked of equality, each was willing enough to share it with those who were above him, but not with those beneath him. "I am the equal of the Montmorencies, but the scavenger is not my equal"—thus thought a great many. An outcry was raised against titles and decorations; after taking them from their possessors, people bedizened themselves with them. How many austere republicans have we seen transformed into chamberlains—how many tribunes created peers of France, who had no scruple to exchange the title of citizen for that of my lord duke or most serene highness!

One day, being on march, an artillery-waggon, drawn by four mules, wanted to cross my regiment; but the soldiers, passing successively before the noses of the poor beasts, took a malicious pleasure in preventing their progress, because they belonged to the imperial guard. At length, one of them cried out in a waggish tone: "Come, soldiers of the line, make way for the mules of the guard."—"Pooh!" replied another, "they are but asses."—"They are mules, I tell you."—"And I tell you they are asses."—"Well, supposing they are asses, what does it signify? Don't you know that in the guard asses have the rank of mules?"

The imperial guard, formed originally of old regiments of grenadiers and chasseurs, had been reinforced by regiments of fusileers, and to these were afterwards added riflemen, voltigeurs, flankers, and pupils. The organization of these corps was wholly exceptional. The old regiments formed part of the old guard, and the others of the young guard. The superior officers and captains had been selected from the first to form the second; they there retained their rank and their prerogatives, while the lieutenants and sub-officers were treated nearly as in the line, excepting the uniform of the guard, which they had the honour to wear. There was consequently an enormous disproportion between the captain and the lieutenant, both as to rank in the army and as to pay. In the regiments of flankers, which wore a green uniform, the captains and superior officers had the blue coat of the old guard, which gave them a motley appearance.

Amidst all these new denominations there is still one wanting. I have often been surprised that the Emperor never conceived the idea of forming a few regiments of *marchers*. I have known in all the corps of the army men who never tired—who could walk thirty or forty successive hours, without taking a moment's rest. By collecting together all these stout-limbed fellows, an excellent regiment might have been composed.

Fancy to yourself two or three thousand picked men, capable of marching two days and two nights without stopping; arm them lightly; let there be neither baggage nor horse to retard their progress or to prevent them from ascending hills; and conceive what services such a body of men might render under certain circumstances. I submit this idea to the gentlemen of the war-office; perhaps it is deserving of their attention.

No man ever knew how to make an army march better than Napoleon. These marches were frequently very fatiguing; sometimes half the soldiers were left behind; but, as they never lacked good-will, they did arrive, though they arrived later. Nothing ruffles the men's temper more than an order vaguely worded, and imperfectly comprehended, which causes them to go over more ground than is necessary; or when any hesitation keeps them for some time on the same spot, uncertain whether they are to remain there or to proceed. A French army is always in good humour when it is fighting; but the best soldiers are done up under the circumstances to which I have just adverted.

Require of them all possible efforts, and they will obey without a murmur; but let the orders be positive, clearly worded, and well delivered. In the contrary case, they will send the general *à tous les diables*. Frederic II. said one day, as M. de Montazet, a general in the Austrian service, then a prisoner in Berlin, who heard him, relates in his Memoirs: "Were I commander of the French, I would make the best troops in the four quarters of the world. To wink at some little thoughtless indiscretions, never to harass them to no purpose, to keep up the natural cheerfulness of their disposition, to be scrupulously just towards them, not to vex them with any minutiæ—such would be my secret for rendering them invincible."

After the campaign of 1809, we were cantoned in the environs of Passau, on mountains covered six feet deep with snow. It was quite a new world, another Siberia. We might have said, like the soldier on the mountains of the Tyrol, who wrote to his parents: "We have got to the end of the world; a hundred paces from our camp, the earth terminates: we can touch the sun with our hands;" only we should have found it the more difficult to touch the sun, because we never saw that luminary. In this charming abode of wolves, the strata of snow, piled one upon another, are frozen so hard, that it is impossible to inter the dead in winter; they are, therefore, laid upon the roofs till a thaw comes. And, gracious heaven! what a thaw! what an ocean of mud! every brook swells to a river, every road is a torrent.

We were very quiet in our villages, when, one fine night, we received orders to start forthwith, and to assemble at Passau. A south wind had been melting the snow for some days; no words can convey any idea of the labour we had to climb and descend all those inundated hills. A painter purposing to represent ascene of the deluge ought to visit that country under similar circumstances. Aides-de-camp, couriers, orderlies, on foot and on horseback, crossed each other in all directions, to hasten such detachments as they should fall in with! We were required to be in Passau, dead or alive, by daybreak. Officers, soldiers, everybody, concluded that hostilities had recommenced. What other motive could be assigned for this precipitate march in time of peace?

As soon as a company, or a fraction of a company, arrived at Passau, officers appointed by the general, embarked it on the Danube, which rolled down mountains of water. The current was so swollen by the melting of the snow, that we had to make a circuit of several leagues to reach the right bank. Artillery-horses fell into the water, boats were upset, men were drowned. Having crossed the Danube, we pursued our route without taking a moment's rest; we marched for forty hours. "But what are we running for in this manner?" said the soldiers. "What has happened that nothing is to stop us—neither night, nor torrents, nor rivers?" In the end, we learned the motives for this forced march, the longest, the most arduous, ever performed, even in time of war: we were going to Braunau, there to pay military honours to Maria Louisa, who was coming to France to marry Napoleon. To see the manner in which we were urged, you would have supposed that the empress was waiting for us: we arrived, in fact, a fortnight too early.

On the frontiers of Bavaria and Austria, near the village

of St. Peter, not far from Braunau, architects from Paris had erected a superb temporary building. Here Maria Louisa was delivered by the plenipotentiaries of the Emperor Francis to those whom Napoleon had appointed to receive her. The Queen of Naples, the Prince of Neufchatel, had arrived with a host of chamberlains, ladies in waiting, equerries, valets of all colours, of all grades, of all kinds. These people are, no doubt, indispensable, for we find crowds of them in all countries, and under all sorts of governments; but, with what these *unbooted* gentry cost him, many a sovereign might set on foot an army of fifty thousand men. When her Majesty appeared, the artillery made an infernal din, the bands of the regiments played false, the drums beat with a dull sound, for the rain fell in torrents; we were up to our knees in mud, and the Paris newspapers were enraptured with the felicity which we had enjoyed of being the first to salute our gracious and august sovereign. Such is the way in which history is written! Next day the Empress set out for Paris; we returned by short marches to our mountains, striving to persuade ourselves that we had been exceedingly amused.

In order to reach the field of battle of Austerlitz, the third corps marched forty leagues in thirty-six hours; that is to say, one twentieth part of the soldiers arrived there, and the rest rejoined them from hour to hour. Officers, left upon the road, picked up the stragglers, and, after a few moments' rest, sent them forward to their regiments. This rapid march was very trying for the soldiers, but they did not complain, because they felt the necessity for it, because it had a great influence on the results of the day. Our trip to Braunau, on the contrary, was with them a perpetual subject of complaint and grumbling. It was the point of comparison, whenever they were harassed to no purpose. "It is somewhat like our march to Braunau," they would say to one another.

The march of thirty-six hours to Austerlitz, without a moment's rest, was of the utmost importance. An officer, who had been taken prisoner, was asked by the Emperor Alexander : "To what corps of the army do you belong ?" —"To the third."—"Marshal Davoust's ?"—"Yes, sire."— "It is not true ; that corps is at Vienna."—"Yesterday it was ; to-day it is here." The Emperor was astounded at this intimation.

Nothing is more fatiguing to the soldier than night-marches : the first necessary for man is sleep. Pichegru paid thirty thousand francs for one night's rest, during which he was apprehended. Sometimes the soldiers slept while marching ; a false step made them roll into a ditch, one over another.

In Bavaria and Austria a great many bees are kept ; and, consequently, there is abundance of wax : the soldiers found great quantities of it in the houses of the peasants. In the night-marches, when the weather was calm, each would light two, three, four, tapers ; nay, some carried so many as fifteen or twenty. Nothing could be more striking than the appearance of a division, thus illuminated, ascending a hill by a winding road ; all those thousands of moving lights presented a most delightful view. Here the jovial fellow of the company sung a sentimental song, which was chorused by all the rest ; there another related the interminable history of La Ramée, who, after quitting the service, came back from the country and travelled two hundred leagues to claim a ration of bread of his sergeant-major. La Bruyère has ascribed to Menalque all the traits of absence of mind that he was acquainted with ; in like manner our soldiers father all the stories of old troopers on La Ramée—he is the type of the French soldier. No soldier of any nation knows how to accommodate himself to his position so well as the French soldier. In the most difficult circumstances a *bon mot* caused everything to be forgotten ; this one soon gave rise to another; presently the air rang with merriment; and the mind, recovering its temper, acquired new energy.

When you see a regiment upon a high road, you think, perhaps, that nothing can be easier than to direct it. At the command, *March!* the men start, you will say, and if they keep marching long enough straight forward, they will be sure to get to their journey's end. If a colonel were to pay no other attention to the men of his regiment, he would leave half of them behind. The sub-officer who marches at the head ought to have a short, regular step; for, if the right goes at the ordinary pace, the left will gallop. The least obstacle that presents itself on the way, were it only a wheel-rut to cross, obliges all the soldiers of the last battalion to run, in order to overtake their comrades. If the first who comes to the obstacle slackens his march but for half a second, the last will have to gallop for a quarter of an hour. An experienced chief sees these things at a glance; he orders a halt for a moment, and all resumes its accustomed course. After marching for an hour, there is a halt of five minutes for lighting pipes, and therefore called the *halt of pipes*. The soldier ought not to be deprived of any pleasure, for to many this pleasure is an absolute want.

At mid-day there is the grand halt, which lasts for an hour; each dines upon what he has in his knapsack, and the march is then resumed, broken by a halt of five minutes after every league.

Little causes frequently produce great effects. Regiments have sometimes been beaten, because the soldiers had no straps to their gaiters. To some, this may look like a joke, but I will explain myself. When the roads are bad, if the soldier is not well shod, if the gaiter does not entirely cover the shoe, the mud finds its way into it, makes the feet sore, occasions blisters; the men fall behind, the ranks are thinned, and the regiment, reduced to one half, cannot be so efficient as if it were complete.

A very important point for an officer is to see that the soldiers have good shoes, and that each of them has in his knapsack gaiter-straps, an awl, and strong thread, to sew them on in case of need. The neglect of this precaution may cause the loss of a battle. The captains, the *chefs de bataillon,* the colonels, are deeply interested in keeping as many men as possible in the ranks; in fact, if they have any commission to execute, if they receive orders to carry a position, to attack a post, the giver of those orders will not consider what number of men they can take with them: the regiment, the battalion, the company, will be required to start; and the more men he has, so much the better for the leader; the business will be done with the greater ease. Thus the glory, the honour, the personal interest, of the officer, imperatively command him to pay incessant attention to these petty details, which may be productive of the most beneficial results to himself. I have seen captains, who, by taking these and other precautions, had kept their companies, when in the field, one fourth stronger than those of others.

In marching in hot weather, the soldiers swallow a great deal of dust, and stop at every well and every stream to drink. What is the consequence? The more they drink, the more thirsty they are; the water, which they swallow in excessive quantity, frequently gives the fever to many of them; and the hospitals are filled to the detriment of the army. This serious inconvenience may be avoided by a very simple expedient, that is, by obliging the men to carry a straw between their lips: their lips being thus closed, the dust cannot get into their mouths; they are not thirsty, and they do not want to drink. I recommend this receipt to persons travelling on foot, and especially to sportsmen.

In order to appreciate all these things, you must live with the soldier, you must see him at all times, you must be with him under all circumstances. The officers of the old *régime* were as brave as those of the new; but, never seeing their soldiers unless on the day of battle, or at reviews held by the king, and returning immediately after to Versailles, they were utter strangers to those minutiæ of high importance. Had they been acquainted with them, I much doubt whether they would have taken the trouble to attend to them; their business was to travel post to the army, the day before it was to fight, and not one of them was missing at the rendezvous.

When a regiment travelled in Germany, the towns through which it passed furnished carriages to convey the baggage, the sick, and the lame. When an officer was going alone, either on a particular mission, or to rejoin his corps, he was provided at each station with a fresh carriage, and, without opening our purses, we had traversed Germany in all directions. At the post stations a carriage was kept ready harnessed, night and day; this was very commodious for us, but it must have been very burdensome to the country.

We travelled post, as you see, at a very cheap rate. At the risk of making enemies of the French postillions, I will tell you an economical method, to which an eccentric acquaintance of mine one day had recourse. You know that the regulations allow the driver seventy-five centimes for every post you travel; nevertheless, when you give him no more than double, he is not satisfied. My acquaintance said to himself at starting: "I will only pay the allowance granted by law, and I will be driven full gallop." His inventive genius supplied him with the following receipt: "My friend," said he to the postillion, who came to drive the first stage, "I am very ill, racked with pains, with rheumatism; the least jolt makes me cry out; you must drive me as gently as possible, or I shall die in the carriage." They started. The postillion avoided the pavement, drove the carriage over the soft ground, took care to keep it in perfect equilibrium, and on reaching the next stage, was presented with a fifteen sous piece, as the reward of all his attentions.

"Surely, sir," said he, "you have made a mistake."

"No mistake whatever."

"But everybody gives at least double."

"Others may do as they please; I pay the allowance."

"But, sir . . . ."

"Read the law of . . . ."

"That law has not common sense."

"For my part I think it extremely sensible."

"Because it is in your favour."

"It is in everybody's favour."

"You will give me something to drink."

"The law mentions nothing of the kind."

"Oh! d—n the law!"

"Let me alone . . . . Oh! my pains are coming again!"

Away went the postillion, grumbling, to find his successor, who was to drive the next stage. Showing him the piece of fifteen sous, "You have got a profitable job," said he, "the allowance and nothing more; nothing to drink; the bare fifteen sous. He knows the law by heart; but, in your turn, you may serve him a trick. The miserly rascal is ill; the least jolt makes him cry out as if he was being flayed alive. He likes to be driven at a foot-pace, and on the soft ground; I was stupid enough to do as he wished, because I expected him to pay handsomely, but he gives the mere allowance. Take him upon the pavement, lash away, drive at full gallop, and if he dies in his carriage . . . so much the better."

His comrade punctually followed his directions; the horses flew like the wind, and the artful traveller laughed in his sleeve. From time to time, in order to encourage the postillion, he shouted to him to stop, to set him down, to slacken his pace; his words were lost in the air; the driver pretended not to hear him, and the carriage dashed away

like lightning. The private directions accompanied him from Paris to Marseilles; the miser was driven like a prince. Luckily the carriage was a strong one.

I was on my way from Warsaw to Posen; the carnival had induced me to stay a few days longer than I should have done in the Polish capital, and I had no more time than was strictly necessary to reach Posen, at the moment mentioned in my instructions, by travelling night and day. On the road I had well nigh been devoured by wolves. The commandant of Lowiez, an officer of the 111th regiment, whom I knew, strove to dissuade me from setting out at nightfall, saying, that the forest of twelve leagues, which I had to pass through, in order to reach Kutno, was full of wolves; that the most imminent danger threatened imprudent travellers, especially in winter; and that those animals had frequently devoured horses and men.* I replied, that if the forest was full of lions and tigers, I should not hesitate to set out. I had committed a fault, and I wished, at any hazard, to keep it from being known. The commandant then offered me a musket and cartridges, for my soldier and myself; his forethought saved our lives.

Scarcely had we proceeded a short league before our sledge was escorted by a regiment of wolves: we saw their eyes glaring like burning coals, and we could plainly distinguish the beasts themselves upon the snow. The position was critical; but I thought that with coolness and steadiness I might extricate myself from it. What gave me most uneasiness was the panic that had seized the peasant who drove the sledge. I said some words to him in Polish, to

* At the beginning of the reign of Louis XIV., a detachment of dragoons was attacked near Pontarlier, in the mountains of the Jura, by an innumerable multitude of wolves. The dragoons fought with courage; they killed several hundred of the animals; but overwhelmed by numbers, they were all devoured, together with their horses. A cross, erected on the spot, with an inscription upon it, recording the event, was still in existence at the commencement of the revolution of 1789.

cheer him up; for, unacquainted with the language, I could not harangue him after the fashion of Homer's heroes. The poor fellow shivered with cold and fright; he lashed his horses, and we went like the wind.

I knew that wolves are afraid of fire: my soldier and I discharged our pieces at them as fast as we could load them; we must have killed many, for our balls, fired upon a dense mass, were sure to hit some one of the greedy animals: but we felt no inclination to go and pick up the dead to fill the game-bag. Several times they approached in close array to within ten paces, but two musket-balls and the flash of the priming ridded us of their presence for a few moments. Had they leaped upon the horses, it would have been all over with us; but, luckily, they contented themselves with howling, like wolves, and following us to the first houses of Kutno, which we once more beheld with inexpressible pleasure. The distance from Lowiez to Kutno is twelve leagues; we performed it in less than three hours: justly may it be asserted that fear gives wings.

In Spain we never travelled singly: the first tree would have served as a gibbet for the imprudent wight who should have ventured alone upon any road. It was necessary to go in bodies, with advanced-guard and rear-guard always in readiness to fire. The governor of Bayonne stopped the detachments and the officers proceeding singly to Spain; and when the whole formed a mass capable of resisting, he permitted them to set out for Irun.

When I crossed the Bidassoa to enter the kingdom of Don Jose primero, sovereign of Spain and the Indies, as he called himself, our convoy consisted of a dozen detachments, belonging to different corps, a great number of single officers rejoining their regiments, persons attached to the commissariat, young men going to Madrid to solicit appointments, and administrators of the *droits réunis* proceeding to Spain to organize it in the same manner as France; for it behoved us to put that country in possession of all the advantages which our supremacy was capable of procuring for it.

At the moment of our departure from Irun, the commander of the convoy regulated the march of this motley assemblage, a task that was none of the easiest. Sixty carriages, drawn by oxen, were laden with the baggage, and marched in the centre; two waggons, with three horses, would easily have carried the whole; but the carts of Biscay are so small that four knapsacks would completely fill one of them. The wheels are of a solid piece, without spokes or fellies, and look like the top and bottom of a butt, with a strong stake run through them, the whole turning together with an infernal creaking. When several of these vehicles are proceeding along the road together, they make a most tremendous clatter, that can only be compared to that of the old machine of Marley.

Between Irun and Hernani, some guerilleros, whom we called brigands, fired a dozen shot at us from the top of the hills; our riflemen soon put them to flight. You should have seen at that moment the pale, wan faces of our Paris fashionables; they hid themselves behind the baggage-carts, when they could not find room enough behind the oxen. Whenever the like circumstance occurred in the sequel, all those who did not wear the uniform separated from the military, with whom they had previously been intermixed, and sought a shelter which did not always protect them. "Why," said I, "are these people afraid? and how is it that the soldiers, who run the same risks as they, never think of danger?" Here is the answer which I gave myself to this question.

It is said that the dress does not make the monk; now I contend that it almost always makes the soldier. Among the military who heard the balls whizzing past, there certainly were many on whom their shrill discordant sound made a disagreeable impression; but, in this case, each is afraid of betraying weakness to his neighbour; he dreads the jeers, the taunts, that would be the inevitable consequences. Duty, honour, pride, all concur to combat fear; and I have often seen the greatest cowards the first to cry: "Forward!" If all those clerks, advocates, auditors, had had the uniform on their backs, if they had formed part of a regiment, if they had been forced to be brave, they would not have dared to show fear, they would not have betrayed in any way their inward emotion. But all this did not in the least concern them; they could tremble at their ease, without being noticed by any one. Their clothes, cut according to the latest Paris fashion, exposed a nicely plaited shirt-bosom; a stray ball might have deranged its elegant disposition, and this unpleasant circumstance they were anxious to avoid. The soldiers cracked their jokes upon them; and very often, to divert themselves at their expense, would tell them that in a quarter of an hour the convoy would be attacked by troops which they had seen stealing along behind the hills: that the best thing that could happen to them would be to get killed in the action; for, if they were taken, they would be sure to be hanged, burned, or flayed. It is certain that, on hearing this language, messieurs the fashionables sincerely wished they had never left France, and they would gladly have renounced all their dreams of ambition to be safe at home again.

The mountain of Salinas was frequently celebrated at that period for the ambuscades which Mina, Longa, and El Pastor were incessantly laying for our convoys. Never was spot more favourable: a mountain which it took four hours to climb, a road bordered by heights and precipices, could not be cleared by the riflemen; the enemy concealed himself behind rocks; you never saw him, but you heard the reports of his musketry, which made some amends. We had the gratification to furnish the subject of a farce and of several pictures exhibited at the Museum, which cannot but be accounted an honour.

We had been ascending for three hours, preceded by our advanced guard, which had not seen anything, when all at once a pistol, discharged close to us, gave the signal to two or three hundred muskets to fire at the same moment. A ravine separated us from the Spaniards; our men immediately set about descending into the valley, with the intention of getting to the other side, but the guerillas had soon disappeared. We lost fourteen men in this affair; a charming woman, the wife of one of the superior *employés* of the hospitals, and who was going to him at Madrid, was wounded by a ball in the breast, and died two days afterwards at Vittoria. The guerillas, however, had not effected their retreat with sufficient celerity to avoid the return made to their fire; three of them were wounded, and presently brought in by the voltigeurs who had gone in pursuit of them: they were carried to Vittoria, and hanged on the following day. One of our dandies was slightly wounded in the leg: thenceforward, proud of his wound, and assuming the air of a little hero, he always kept among the grenadiers, disdaining the society of his former companions; it seemed as though he meant to punish them for not having been so lucky as himself.

But, in travelling in Spain, we were obliged to make frequent halts. At each town some portion of the convoy found themselves at the place of their destination; the column, thus weakened, needed fresh reinforcements before it could pursue its route. Half, nay, I may say, almost the whole of the French army, was occupied in escorting couriers; we had garrisons in all the towns and in all the villages upon the high roads: and very often midway between them there had been erected little forts, block-houses, redoubts, each occupied by perhaps a hundred soldiers.

All these posts, all these garrisons, furnished a greater or less number of men for escorts, according to the presumed force of the bands of insurgents that were in the environs. This service was extremely arduous, and it may be affirmed that it caused the death of more Frenchmen than the most sanguinary pitched battles. We were masters of all the towns and villages upon the road, but not of the environs at the distance of one hundred paces. It was a war of every day, of every hour. If the escort was numerous and well commanded, it met with nobody in its way; in the contrary case, the enemy appeared on every side of us: it may be said that in Spain he was everywhere and nowhere.

The reports that reached us, respecting his force and his movements, were scarcely ever true; whereas he was apprized, day by day, hour by hour, of what we were doing: we were counted in every village, and the enemy's leaders always knew which was our weak side. A colonel, on arriving in a town, demanded two thousand four hundred rations for his regiment. "You have eighteen hundred and sixty men," replied the alcalde; "you shall have no more than eighteen hundred and sixty rations: they are ready for you."

The profession of spy in the army is a very dangerous one; and, to get well served by men who every day run the risk of the gallows, a general ought to pay liberally. The government transmitted to the commanders-in-chief considerable sums for this purpose. But several of them were niggardly in the expenditure of this money. To obtain services which the prospect of gain alone can induce a man to render, they preferred terror. After imprisoning the wife and children of a poor fellow, they would say to him:—"You must be gone immediately, and get back to-morrow, and tell me all that Mina, Longa, El Pastor [or whoever it might be] is doing; what is his force, his position. If you deceive me, or fail to return, I will order your whole family to be hanged."

What was the consequence? The peasant did not come

back, and not a creature was hanged; or, perhaps, he went and told all he knew to Mina, who gave him his cue, and so contrived it that the truth one day was a falsehood on the morrow. The money allowed for secret services, for the pay of spies, was sent back to Paris, and matters went on most prosperously—according to the bulletins.

Though the Spanish nation had risen *en masse* against us, though it was waging a national war with us, yet, by paying liberally, we should have found traitors. The love of country was not the sole motive of the insurrection; it had furnished the pretext for it—that was all. Most of the guerillas, when they found nothing to do against the French, plundered their own countrymen: all were alike to them. They thought only of enriching themselves, leaving the country to settle its business as it best might. This course is not a novelty: we find it in all countries, in all ages, in time of peace, as well as in time of war.

In many villages the peasants called both the French and the guerillas brigands. When I one day asked an alcalde:—" Is it long since you had the brigands in this part of the country?" he inquired: " Which do you mean?—the French or the Spaniards?"

In proof of what I am asserting, I may adduce the celebrated Chacarito. This chief of a band, after making war upon the French, turned his arms against the Spaniards in his leisure moments, in order to keep his hand in. He had struck such terror into Castile, that the Spaniards had joined the French to endeavour to take him. Betrayed by one of his men, he was seized in a *venta*, which he defended like a lion. A few days afterwards he suffered the most horrible of deaths in the public place of Valladolid. Quartered by four horses, his disparted members were placed on wheels at the four cardinal points of the city; but this example did not deter other brigands from pursuing the same course.

For the rest, these bands fled before a few riflemen: unless greatly superior in number, they would not dare to attack us boldly; and, in this case, they had the immense advantage of surprising us in ambuscades. The country is so broken by mountains and precipices, that it is impossible to guard the roads properly. When a chief of guerillas had come back from an expedition, his whole band dispersed, the arms were hidden, and each returned to his home, after agreeing to meet again on such a day, perhaps twenty or thirty leagues off. The French set out in pursuit of them; they did not meet with a creature; and the Paris newspapers proclaimed to all Europe that such or such a general had, with an intrepidity deserving the highest admiration, driven the brigands into their mountains; that they were a cowardly crew, unworthy to bear arms, &c., &c. But all these fine official phrases did not prevent the brigands, as they were termed, from assiduously pursuing their vocation. By harassing us incessantly, they fatigued our men, who fell ill: they occupied half the army in protecting couriers, and very frequently a battalion was not sufficient to escort a letter.

The great art in partisan warfare is always to attack, and never be forced to accept battle. The guerillas made it their study not to be found when we looked for them; to pounce upon us like vultures when we least expected them; and it must be confessed that they completely performed their task. Sometimes it happened that they were hanged when taken in arms: this was the dark side of their profession, the reverse of the medal; but they served the French who fell into their power in the same manner; nay, they frequently carried their reprisals to the most revolting barbarity. On several occasions they flayed alive the prisoners whom the fortune of war had thrown into their hands: many of those miserable wretches were sawed asunder between two planks; one of my friends was buried alive in the ground, all but his head, which served as a mark for the savages to play at bowls. One might fill volumes with the atrocities committed on both sides in this graceless war; but I can affirm, without fear of being contradicted by any one, that we were always less cruel than the Spaniards.

It is astonishing what a quantity of indulgences may be earned on a march in Spain. In the towns, in the villages, on the high roads, you find saints and virgins set up in niches. You read underneath, in large letters:—" One thousand years'—two thousand years'—ten thousand years' indulgences for every one who will say five Paters and five Aves before this holy image."

In Spain the Christian religion has sunk to that point at which paganism had arrived among the Romans. With the major part of the Spanish people, a saint, a Virgin of gold and silver, is the object of adoration. The devotee kneels before the image, sees but that, and conceives no higher thought. Remove the statue, and all is gone; if you set up another, it will have no efficacy. The old one wrought miracles, and, till its successor has performed at least a dozen, it will be thought nothing of. The Spaniards have confined Christianity to ceremonies: they think that they have done all that can be done, when they have fasted, worn the scapulary, and read mechanically so many pages of a book.

According to their notions, religion cannot exist without monks and processions: they must have relics, and miracles, and ecclesiastics in grotesque dresses, and convents, where every one may find prayers and soup. In religion, they are materialists, without being aware of it; in love they are materialists, and they acknowledge it. In regard to everything else, they are happy after they have satisfied their material wants: this is proved to demonstration.

They have a respect for God, but one may affirm that they show a much greater for the saints: each village has its patron, whom they invoke, and to whom alone they pray. The Virgin shares the honours paid to the saints of each particular place or district. It is to her that a Spanish female appeals to witness the truth of what she affirms; it is in the name of the Virgin that she swears constancy to her lover, that she promises to meet him. The Spaniards think nothing of God; they very seldom mention his name. A peasant one day said in my presence: "At Matapasuelos there is a saint who has as much power as God."—"And a great deal more," added another.

You cannot invent a story so absurd, so silly, so stupid, as that a Spanish monk shall not be able to make his countrymen believe it. Such a saint has shed tears, such a Virgin has moved her arms, her foot, her head; everybody believes it, because a man in black has told them so. Presently, every one affirms that he has seen it: how is it possible afterwards to doubt a thing which the whole town maintains to be true! Voltaire somewhere says, that if twenty thousand men were to come before him and swear that they had seen a dead person come to life, he would not believe them. Voltaire was quite right; for, in every village in Spain, you may find plenty of people who would affirm that they beheld this miracle.

On my arrival at Burgos, I went to see the magnificent cathedral. My cicerone told me that at the hospital they would show me a Christ on the cross, whose nails grew so fast that it was necessary to cut them every week. I went, therefore, to the hospital to see the crucifix. The keeper was absent, but I was shown the man whose office it is to perform every week the chirurgical operation.

This reminds me of the story of a poor devil, who, to get a few sous from the cockneys of Paris, had installed himself in a booth on the Boulevard. After sounding the trumpet and beating the drum to collect the simpletons, " Walk in, gentlemen," said he, "to see this rare and curious animal; he has travelled all over the four quarters of the world, namely, Europe, Asia, Africa, and Norway. Never was his like before seen; he is the offspring of the incestuous loves of a carp and a rabbit; and, what is most astonishing, gentlemen, the carp is the father." The gaping fools paid their two sous and entered the booth. "Gentlemen," said the confederate of the barker, "Monsieur the Count de Lacepède, grand chancellor of the Legion of Honour, and director of the Museum of Natural History, has this very moment sent for the animal, for the purpose of drawing up a report concerning it for the Emperor Napoleon. I cannot, therefore, show it to you to-day, but you shall see the father and mother." Then, for his two sous, the cockney gazed at leisure at a rabbit in a cage and a carp in a pail of water.

Many women followed their husbands to the army, either because from conjugal affection they would not be parted from them, or because their circumstances did not allow them to keep two establishments. When we took the field, however, they remained at the depôt; but, as soon as peace was made, they arrived by carriage-loads. These ladies travelled in cabriolets, in calèches, in carts; their chaste ears must often have been shocked by the language which they heard; and, at every halt, their eyes must have encountered objects still more hideous. In Germany, these ladies, who followed the army, lived in a very comfortable manner; they were in no sort of danger: but, in Spain, the case was totally different. In travelling along the road, they were, like us, exposed to the fire of musketry; and when their escort, falling into an ambuscade, left them to the mercy of the Spanish brigands, they underwent the most infamous usage.

In a skirmish near Burgos, the wife of an officer of my acquaintance had her carriage broken in pieces, and she was forced to proceed sorrowfully on foot. She was soon overwhelmed with fatigue; the perspiration trickled down her face; her delicate limbs could no longer support their burden; it was impossible for her to go a hundred paces farther. Her husband was extremely distressed to see his wife in such a condition.

"Poor Laura!" said he to me, "she will certainly die upon the road, if I cannot meet with a carriage, a horse, or a mule, to carry her."

"We shall not find any to-day, but I think I observed in the rear-guard a soldier driving an ass, and if you can prevail on him to sell or lend it you . . . ."

"An excellent thought! you are my best friend, that you are. Where is that soldier? where is that ass? I would give fifty louis for an ass; I must have an ass for Laura. Poor Laura, how tired she is!"

"She cannot stir another step."

"I would give a hundred louis for an ass. Money was made to circulate; and of what benefit is it to have money if Laura suffers? Let us go and look for this ass."

"I dare say you might get it at a much cheaper rate."

"What signifies the price, so I do but find an ass! But where shall we find one?"

"At the rear-guard. I think it belongs to some marauder, who is keeping out of the way. Let the regiment pass on; we shall soon see."

"Courage, Laura; walk a little farther; I shall soon be back."

The column had by degrees passed us. The rear-guard appeared, and we saw a voltigeur leading by the bridle a long-eared animal, upon which he had slung his knapsack on one side, and his musket as a counterpoise, on the other.

"Aha! there is the ass that we are looking for!—I say, voltiguer, my wife is ill; she cannot walk any farther; you must sell me that ass."

"That I will, captain."

"How much do you ask for it?"

"Twenty francs."

"Are you joking? Twenty francs! twenty francs! and for a stolen ass—for you have stolen it—and it would serve you right if I were to inform the general-in-chief."

"But, captain, I did not steal it; I found it as we were passing through the last village."

"You *found* it, did you? I am not such a simpleton as to believe that."

"But, even if I had stolen it, you ought to be very glad, since you are in want of such a thing."

"Well, I will give you two pieces of one hundred sous for your ass."

"Oh, no! I must have twenty francs."

"Well, take your choice between my two hundred sous and a complaint to the general-in-chief."

"Here, take my ass."

"My dear fellow," said he, turning to me, "it is horribly dear—ten francs for a stolen ass! but, never mind, money was made to circulate."

EDITOR'S REMARKS

ON

CHAPTER III.

THERE is little to observe upon in the third chapter; still, a few remarks may be made on these amusing stories, as my chief object is to exhibit the difference between foreign armies and the British army, whether favourable to our troops or otherwise.

1st. The difference between the imperial guards of France and her Majesty's guards in England, is striking: the imperial guards were, as ours are, highly favoured; but unlike ours, they earned that favour by severe service. They had, individually and collectively, done more than the troops of the line. Ours have done less. There is not a regiment of the British line which has any cause to feel itself inferior to the guards in merit. Many hold the guards to be inferior.

This is prejudice; the truth being that, with regard to merit, all regiments are upon a par. In the general course of service, each may be at times better, and, at times, worse, than its neighbour, according to the abilities of its commanding officer, and the place where it is quartered. No quarters are more trying, and more likely to injure discipline, than London and Windsor, where the guards are usually quartered. The men are tempted night and day, and the black book of the household troops is no criterion by which to judge of their comparative merit. I should say that the guards might have more punishment than most regiments, and yet be in as good, or better, order.

But with great admiration for the regiments of guards as fine bodies of men, ever ready to do their work in battle as becomes British soldiers, still they do not do the hard work of the service like other regiments. The British army is different from every other. Our real hard trial is colonial service, and the guards do not take that. Nor do they form a body of men chosen for individual merit. Were such the case, it would render their peculiar privileges unobjectionable to the line. It does not appear that the Emperor Napoleon favoured the officers of the Imperial Guard by an undue proportion of command as general officers. His favour seems to have been bestowed upon them as a corps, and (according to the French soldier) of the asses he made mules; but there he stopped.

2nd. The observations made upon the French republicans are very good. Many of those gentlemen are alive, and may defend their conduct against the sarcasms of the writer, if they can. I believe that Carnot remained the most free from reproach; but, able as he was, and honest as he is said to have been, he acted in conjunction with the assassins of the "Reign of Terror," and finally he took the title of "Count" from Napoleon. How republican giants dwindled into pigmies, in the hands of that commanding mind! The first must remain a stain upon Carnot's character for ever. The last, as he pretended to be a "stern republican," was pitiable or laughable, or what the reader pleases. Republicans are fond of being "stern." One was "stern," and put his own son to death. Another was "stern," and assassinated his benefactor, if not his father; being a usurer, he was also "stern," especially with his debtors, so stern as to starve a cityful; for Brutus did these things by wholesale, just as the French republicans used grape-shot at Lyons. Sometimes Whigs, Tories, and Radicals, are "stern path-of-duty men," as Cobbett called them. But why men should pique themselves on being truculent instead of just I know not; but so it is, that republicans seem to rejoice (to use a newspaper word) in the title of "stern." Malesherbes was not stern, though he was bold, when he defended Louis XVI., yet posterity will hold his character in higher estimation than that of the "stern" Carnot. Men should be stern to their enemies, but not to their countrymen; and, above all, not to those who are in their power. To be called "stern path-of-duty men" seems to gratify some men; they seem to consider it as a virtue: so the men described by M. Blaze were, no doubt, stern republicans, till the great Napoleon came, who was, I may say, bred in a republic; but no sooner did he get power enough to save his head from the guillotine, than he put an end to all that bloody work, and *sterns* were turned into *prows*, or at least, *figure-heads*, bedecked with coronets. Finally, they have finished by being objects of ridicule to the writer and other sensible men; and, in a few years more, will only be remembered, as other executioners are, by those who rummage history to find out the disgusting transactions of the age.

3rd. The horrors committed by the French and Spaniards in the Spanish war are recounted by the author with a just feeling of disgust. I believe he is right in saying that the Spaniards were the worst of the two nations; and I also believe that the latter *began* the infamous cruelties inflicted upon the prisoners. However, one thing every English officer knows, namely, that both the British and French armies behaved like honourable soldiers to each other; and the former protected the French prisoners from the cruelty of the Spaniards as much as was in their power. I speak generally. There might have been a few infamous exceptions: but I never myself witnessed anything so disgraceful to military and national honour as the maltreatment of a prisoner of war by *military* men.

I will not say the same of the Transport Office in England, whose treatment of the French prisoners appeared to me to be absolutely dreadful. The whole government was implicated in this detestable affair, from the effect of which, numbers, it is said, became idiots. The idea of shutting up honourable soldiers, who were prisoners of war, in the hulks of ships for years, a punishment far beyond that inflicted on the most infamous felons, who are only shut up for a few months, is too painful to any honourable man to speak of without expressing his abhorrence of it. It was disgraceful to the government of those days, and forms a strong contrast to the honourable treatment which the English prisoners received in France, by order of the Emperor Napoleon: at least, I have never heard that, as a body, British officers or soldiers who were prisoners complained of the treatment received: individuals may, but we have only *their* story. We were told that the French prisoners *were so numerous* that it was necessary to confine them in hulks. This was an idle excuse. What was to hinder these honourable and brave men from being placed in one or two of our Western Islands, which they would have cultivated, and whence they could not have escaped, if we had forbidden all boats to approach the islands, save an armed vessel or two to guard the coast? This was proposed at the time, but there was in those days a desire to insult the French, which prevented this humane, honourable, and useful proposal from being received: and the cruel expedient of shutting brave men up in those floating prisons for years, exposed to everything horrible, was adopted. No honest British soldier will ever speak of this matter without expressing his detestation of such conduct towards prisoners of war.

Now to return from this long digression, which I made from necessity, because, whenever I think of the Transport Office, and the ill-treatment which the French prisoners received, and compare it with the kind treatment which I myself, and all who were with me, received from Marshals Soult and Ney, it gives me such a fit of spleen that I must necessarily give vent to it; the reader will, therefore, pardon me, in consideration of the physical necessity by which I am impelled.

All the horrors committed by the French and Spanish soldiers upon each other, and upon women and children, are hateful, as are all the cruelties of a similar nature perpetrated in the East Indies and in the colonies. All these horrors are fairly and justly laid to the charge of Napoleon in one case, and of British ministers in the other. It is in vain that sophistry and national prejudice endeavour to throw off from the shoulders of an English government the responsibility for crimes committed in an unjust war. Napoleon was the author of the Spanish aggressions. The English were the aggressors in India; and, although our sovereign can do no wrong, his ministers can, and no man can lay a heavier charge upon Napoleon, than rests upon the English ministers who conquered India and Australia, and protected those who there committed atrocities equal to any recounted by our author. There is one thing to be said, however—that Napoleon was tempted by the folly of the reigning monarch of Spain: his wish, if it had been accomplished, would have promoted the happiness of Spain; he had nothing vile or cruel in his object. Whereas, the object of the English government was to enrich a parcel of shopkeepers; the "shopocracy of England," as it has been well termed; and a more base and cruel tyranny never wielded the power of a great nation. Our object in conquering India, the object of all our cruelties, was *money—lucre :* a thousand millions sterling are said to have been squeezed out of India in the last sixty years. Every shilling of this has been picked out of blood, wiped, and put into the murderers' pockets; but, wipe and wash the money as you will, the "damned spot" will not "out." There it sticks for ever, and we shall yet suffer for the crime as sure as there is a God in heaven, where the "commercial interests of the nation" find no place, or heaven is not what we hope and believe it to be! Justice and religion are mockeries in the eyes of "a great manufacturing country," for the true god of such a nation is Mammon. I may be singular, but, in truth, I prefer the despotic Napoleon to the despots of the East India Company. The man ambitious of universal power generally rules to do good to subdued nations. But the men ambitious of universal peculation rule only to make themselves rich, to the destruction of happiness among a hundred millions of people. The one may be a fallen angel; the other is a hell-born devil!

The English must be a noble people that can do the evil things we have done, and yet be the first nation in the world! We are so grand and so good that, like a powerful ship, which bears being heavily laden, we can carry a vast cargo of sin, and yet sail better than the whole fleet. But to add to our honesty will do us no harm; our mediation between America and France, in 1836, will never do us discredit, nor injure our prosperity : there is something that warms the heart when a man can feel that his country has done a great and noble action. I like better to think of our mediation between France and America than to think of the eternal disgrace which we incurred by sending the Emperor Napoleon to St. Helena.

CHAPTER IV.

QUARTERS—GERMANY, POLAND.

In general, the places that we liked best were precisely those that we quitted soonest, and *vice versa*. It was very rarely indeed that superior orders were in accordance with our pleasures. A person travelling post changes his apartment every day, and sees nothing. I know one who passed through Florence on a fine moonlight night, and exclaimed, with the utmost satisfaction: "Another city seen!" Though marching quickly, we always lodged with people whom we had opportunities to study. One day in a mansion, the next in a cottage, we saw much more of the inhabitants of a country than he who leaves one inn to go to another. In this chapter the reader will find some observations on manners, made on the spot, from day to day, in the different countries that we visited. It is by lodging with people, by eating and drinking with them, by associating with them, that you learn to know them.

Soldiers, travelling in France, are furnished with a billet of lodging, which gives them a right to a place at the fire and the candle: for this reason our Romans of the Empire preferred Germany to France. Among those good Germans they found their dinner ready; their pay remained untouched, and could, therefore, be applied to other purposes—*schnapps,* tobacco, and the like. In Spain they were frequently worse off than in France; they found in their lodgings neither fire nor candle.

In order to obtain good fare the soldiers had recourse to a singular expedient. Lodging several of them together, they agreed what parts to play before they entered the peasant's house. One of them pretended to be in a furious passion: he would swear, storm, draw his sword, and threaten everybody. The women were frightened, ay, and sometimes the men too. His comrades strove to soothe him, and declared that he was the best fellow in the world with those who knew how to humour him; and presently they pointed out his weak side.

"He is fond of good eating and good wine, you must know; that is his hobby. When he is furnished with what he likes, he is as gentle as a lamb, as a new-born infant; but when you give him nothing but potatoes to eat, and sour beer to drink, he is terrible; none of us, nay, not all of us together, should then be able to prevent him from doing some mischief or other. Why, no longer ago than yesterday, about eight leagues off, this real devil set fire to the house of a peasant who carried his incivility to such a length as to put water into the wine that he gave us. We ought not to say so, perhaps; but, after all, our comrade was not so much to blame, for it is wrong to cheat anybody. Consider . . . look about you . . . do things conscientiously . . . let the dinner be nice, the drink good, and all will be right, we will answer for it."

Such speeches, amplified and commented on by the party, usually made a deep impression: the host cheerfully produced his best; our fellows desired nothing more, and all passed off extremely well. These scenes were sometimes performed by officers, though opportunities for this rarely occurred, as they were seldom quartered so many together as to be able to distribute the parts.

We were not liked in Germany; very far from it. The passage or stay of French regiments was an enormous burden to the country. But, though the people abhorred our army in mass, they were fond of us, individually. The jovial, frank, and open character of the French, easily conciliated the friendship of the good Germans, who are in general serious. Notwithstanding the antipathies of nation against nation, it was rare that, an hour after his arrival, the French soldier, who would take any trouble to please, was not as great a favourite as if his host had known him for ten years. Do as they do; smoke, drink beer, and the Germans will be fond of you. And then, such pains had been taken to make them believe the French to be devils, that, when they found they had to deal with well-bred men, they spared nothing to express the joy which they felt.

In Spain, the people liked individuals no better than masses. In a general insurrection, a Spaniard would have cut the throat of a Frenchman sleeping under his roof; a German would have saved him. Almost everywhere in Germany I was kindly received; almost everywhere I was requested to come again, if chance should bring me that way. A soldier, however, ought not to construe these invitations too literally: they are forms of civility which are offered to him at his departure—nothing more. One day I took it in my head to call again upon an honest German: he did not know me; I was obliged to tell my name, my christian name, my age, and quality; in consequence, your humble servant vowed that he would never more place himself in so awkward a predicament.

Once settled in quarters, every one, officer, subaltern, or private, set about paying court to the mistress of the house, or to her daughter, if she had one. My captain was married, but he often forgot this: I have known many officers, who, under certain circumstances, had no more memory than if they had been dipped in Lethe. In all our lodgings he passed himself off for a bachelor. The moment he spied a young female, he began to say sweet things to her, talked of marriage, and now and then he was listened to. Marriage!—there is magic, you know, in that word for a young female; many a man whom she would not deign to look at as a man, she regards with kindness as soon as she believes him to be susceptible of becoming a husband.

Be that as it may, my captain gained a hearing by means

of this petty stratagem; while I, who had always a declaration ready, but did not look like a marrying man, was very often repulsed with loss, though I was twenty years younger than my rival. The respect which I have always professed for good morals, for conjugal fidelity, and, perhaps, also a spice of jealousy, suggested to me an expedient for supplanting him.

As soon as my Lothario began to play the gallant, "Captain," said I to him, aloud, "the *vaguemestre** is just arrived; I dare say he has a letter for you from your wife."

"Hold your tongue," he replied in a whisper. But I pretended not to comprehend him, and rattled away.

"Your Napoleon [all officers' sons were named Napoleon] must be a great boy by this time; he is, no doubt, forward in his learning; he always was an intelligent child. Is he still at the Lyceum of Antwerp?"

"What is that to you?"

"And little Hortense," [all officers' daughters were then named Hortense; subsequently they were called Marie Louise] "is little Hortense as frolicsome as ever?"

"Have done! have done! that does not concern you."

"Upon my word, it must be a pleasant thing to be married, and to have children: this bachelor's life is frequently very wearisome, and I never felt more disposed to give it up than to-day."

The young lady immediately showed more coldness in her answers to the captain; presently she did not even look at him; he was married, consequently he was a useless being. All the ground that he lost, I gained by degrees; and sometimes I had reason to congratulate myself on these indiscretions.

* The *vaguemestre* is a subaltern, who goes to the post-office to fetch the letters for the regiment, and delivers them according to their addresses—in short, a military postman.

"Why, the devil," said he to me, when we were alone, "do you come and talk to me every moment about my wife? I really believe you do it on purpose."

"Certainly."

"But don't you know that it is very wrong?"

"Do you think it is right to violate the vow you made to your wife at the altar? to strive to seduce a young female, by making her believe that you will marry her? Is not this frightful?—and then the morality of the thing!"

"Morality! morality! Do you imagine that you impose upon me with your pretensions to high principles? I see clearly that all your annoyance is but a cunning manœuvre to get into my place."

"It is possible."

"And will morals be a greater gainer by you than by me?"

"It is possible again; for, at any rate, I can marry; you cannot."

"But you will do no such thing."

"How do you know? For some time past, I have felt within me a certain vocation for matrimony; an idea, a whim, may decide me. If I were to see a good example, perhaps I might follow it. You know the story of Panurge's sheep, which, because the leader jumped into the water, all plunged in after it. Besides, you have the advantage of rank over me; allow me that which I have over you. Whenever there are two damsels, you shall have a right to court one of them; but when our host has but one daughter, recollect that to me alone belongs the right of making love to her. I am the younger, and gallantry is in an inverse ratio to military service."

A few days afterwards, we had just arrived at Magdeburg, when I went to see my captain. I found him with a face a yard long: he was sadly heaving deep sighs, mingled with very energetic interjections.

"What is the matter?" said I to him. "Something seems to have ruffled you to-day."

"The matter, my dear fellow! the matter! I will tell you. The fun is at an end . . . Hymen is coming."

"What am I to understand by those words?"

"My wife is coming to join me. I have received notice to that effect this morning."

"Well, captain, accept my most sincere congratulations on the pleasure . . . the felicity . . . which . . ."

"Thank you, thank you; you are pleased to be facetious but I should like to see you in the same predicament."

The Germans were not fond of lodging married officers; their ladies were, in general, extremely troublesome: as they wished to pass for *well-bred* women, they always affected to be dissatisfied, either with the lodging or with the diet, in order to induce a belief that they lived in much better style at the paternal home. During the Restoration, the officers on duty at the Tuileries dined at the palace; it was the fashion in the royal guard to find fault with the fare: a man gave himself the air of a person of consequence by insinuating that it was far inferior to what he had at home. I know not how the kitchens of those gentlemen were organized; but, for my part, when I compared my father's table with that of the Tuileries, I gave the decided preference to the latter.

Wherever I have been quartered, my host has assured me that he would rather have ten soldiers than one officer's wife. In Germany, people liked better to have four Frenchmen quartered upon them than one German of the Confederation of the Rhine. The Bavarians, the Westphalians, the Wurtembergers, were intractable; they began by administering blows with the flat of the sword, and sometimes they went still farther; whereas, the French almost always stopped short at threats.

The King of Wurtemberg had imposed a singular tax in

his dominions. Every female who took the unwarrantable liberty of producing a child without being married was obliged to pay a fine; and this fine brought one hundred thousand dollars per annum into the coffers of his Wurtemberg majesty. Small profits ought not to be neglected. This money was appropriated to the royal kitchen. The grand-master of this essential part of a good government exercised the control over all children born without the sanction of the clergy. A hint this for the governments of other countries. In France, for example, there are born annually about seventy thousand natural children; lay a tax on all these brats. Such a tax would not be vexatious, for it is an established fact that people can live without having children; it would be essentially moral, because it would impel to marriage those who feel a decided vocation for the propagation of their species. I exhort our ministers to consider this suggestion.

After lodging one day with a cobbler, we found ourselves, perhaps, on the morrow in a palace. This was actually the case in the environs of Ulm. Prince Henry of Wurtemberg was exiled by the king, his father; till he should be reinstated in his favour, he led a jovial life at the castle of Wippling. His highness sent us an invitation to dine with him; we accepted it, as officers never fail to do.

The prince drank nothing but champagne; from the beginning of the dinner to the dessert, it was poured out in bumpers; we thought this a strange fashion at first, but we soon got used to it. National spirit contributed to reconcile us to it; for the benefit of the vine-growers of Champagne, we encouraged the consumption. Many other wines were on the table, but the prince touched none of them; they were for us alone; and the prince did the honours with great condescension.

One of the guests at this dinner was a Bavarian officer. I soon perceived that this brave man wore on his left thumb a gold ring of extraordinary dimensions; it was at least four times as large as his finger. A black ribbon, tied round his wrist, held it in its place. But is it a ring? said I to myself. If it is not a ring, what is it then? I had never seen one of such size, and placed in such a manner. All dinner-time, my attention was engrossed by the monster ring; scarcely could the champagne effect from time to time a little diversion. Had I been obliged to go to bed without satisfying my curiosity, I should certainly not have been able to sleep.

I determined, therefore, to seek an explanation. On leaving the table, I approached the officer for the purpose of beginning a conversation. We had made the same campaigns, we had been in the same battles, fighting for the same cause, and we soon got acquainted. We began to talk of professional matters; but I kept my eyes fixed upon the ring.

"Sir," said I, at last, "may I, without indiscretion, ask you what you call the thing which you wear on your left thumb?"

"Don't you see? it is a ring."

"It is very large."

"Yes, that is the reason why I fasten it by the ribbon tied round my wrist."

"But, pardon me, how happens it that you wear a ring of such calibre?"

"Because, in my house, all the seniors have worn it from time immemorial. It was made expressly for one of my ancestors, Otto von Ringelbaum: judge what a man he must have been, and how we are degenerated."

Taking off the ring, he showed it to me. Resembling those large brass rings by which our curtains are suspended, it was of massive gold, and weighed at least a pound.

"Sir," said I, "you have more patience than I should have, for this must be very troublesome."

"Yes, it is troublesome, for it is very heavy; but, you see, all my ancestors wore it, and I must do so too. It is even a privilege which my family enjoys, which I cannot, I ought not, renounce."

"And you are perfectly right."

Among the sovereigns whom accident and my billet procured me the honour of closely observing, I must place in the first rank the Duke of Anhalt-Dessau. That excellent prince united the qualities of the scholar and the courtier with the patriarchal manners of the German burghers. No French officer quitted Dessau without feelings of gratitude for the kind reception that he had experienced. It is in Germany alone that you still find that antique good-nature, that unaffected politeness proceeding from the heart, that frankness in the language as well as in the face of the host.

The moment we had uttered the name of Worlitz, the prince gave orders to his officers to conduct us thither. We knew those celebrated gardens from some verses of Delille's, which I repeated. This seemed to please the duke: he immediately placed carriages, horses, everything, at our disposal.

This was, certainly, the most pleasant excursion that ever I made in my life. Nothing can be more beautiful, more delicious, than the park of Worlitz. Nature and the fine arts have vied in its embellishment: all that refined taste, all that imagination can devise is there, in the compass of a few square leagues. The lawn, as you enter, of immense extent, with a stream running through it, presents an enchanting prospect, with its bridges, sometimes of elegant, at others of grotesque forms; here are flowers, there cascades, yonder rocks, farther on obelisks, statues, museums.

You lose yourself in a shrubbery, on emerging from which you find yourself before a temple with Corinthian columns: this is the library. Beyond it is a farm, with its appropriate animals, utensils, and labourers. A dairy of white marble is managed by young females suitably clad. You would fancy yourself at the Opera. Still farther on, is another edifice of the noblest architecture; this is the cabinet of medals; and beyond it is the picture-gallery. In short, Worlitz is to the Duke of Anhalt-Dessau what to us would be our museums, our library, our cabinet of natural history, collected in a magnificent park.

In passing through the duchy of Anhalt-Dessau, we felt a vague desire to live there for good; on seeing the prince who then governed it we should cheerfully have submitted to all his laws, without demanding of him the guarantees of a representative government. He was a good father amidst his children; they never asked why their sovereign did this or that, knowing that he could do no other than right.

This happy country is not so large as many a department of France, but it is one vast garden. All the roads are bordered on each side by three rows of cherry trees; these present a magnificent sight in the month of June, when they are laden with fruit, from which is made a prodigious quantity of *kirschwasser*.

A fondness for gardens is, indeed, general in Germany; every one, from the prince to the petty shopkeeper, has his own, which he is continually embellishing. The cities, which formerly were fortified, have converted their old bastions into clumps of lilac, their curtains into alleys of flowers, their muddy ditches into handsome pieces of water, studded with islets. Leipzig and Bremen may be mentioned as models of this kind: you may walk round those cities all the way under fine trees, and through alleys of flowers.

These fortifications, converted into pleasure-grounds, presented of themselves inequalities of surface, which, under the management of men of taste, look most delightful. The prospect changes at every step; you have always something fresh to see. This is not like our symmetrical promenades in France, where you have seen everything as soon as you have reached the end of one of the alleys.

A country in which we fared very well and very ill is Poland: there you meet with indigence and luxury at every step. The filthiness of the villages is frightful: in every peasant's dwelling there is a room, or rather a stable, where horses, cows, pigs, and poultry, pass the night: one-fourth of this room is occupied by a prodigious stove, which serves as a bed for the family. The father, the mother, the daughter, and the son-in-law, here sleep all together, on straw laid upon the stove, and everything is transacted there nearly the same as among a herd of swine. Quit this hovel, where you leave human nature in its primitive state, go to the mansion, and you will there find all the refinements of civilization—a select library, all the politeness of well-educated people, agreeable conversation, in short, all the comforts that it is possible to possess in Poland. A journey in that country is a perpetual series of contrasts.

The Polish nobility, in fact, pass in general eleven months of the year at their country-seats. They live there in a very economical manner; but they compensate themselves by the indulgences of the carnival and the feast of St. John, when they go to Warsaw, Posen, or Cracow. There each pursues a ruinous round of dissipation: dinners and entertainments succeed one another from day to day; the streets are thronged with superb equipages; extravagantly high play takes place; at length, the travellers return home, and seek to restore the equilibrium of their finances by making their peasants toil.

This country life is not very agreeable in Poland: each family is confined to its own village; the roads are execrably bad, and there is no such thing as visiting, unless in summer or in severe frost. I would not advise professors of gastronomy to go to Poland in the expectation of realizing there the sublime meditations of Brillat-Savarin. Nowhere but in the towns is there either butcher or baker: a gentleman must have at his own mansion all that is subservient to animal life. He has an ox killed, which supplies his family with fresh meat for three days, and salted beef for three months: and so it is with everything else. Bread can scarcely be reckoned among the necessaries of life for the Poles: all their dishes are seasoned with pastes, flour, or meal. Their ordinary drink is beer of bad quality: in many mansions where I have dined, I have seen but one glass in the middle of a table, and each emptied it in turn. I have seen beautiful, elegant, well-bred young ladies, drink after a nasty, dirty, long-bearded steward, without any repugnance. Accordingly, as soon as I became acquainted with the habits of these people, I procured a goblet, which I reserved for my own separate use.

In Poland I have seen young ladies who had the strange habit of sticking very black pear-pips upon their faces: these looked somewhat like the *mouches* with which our ladies formerly tattooed themselves, and served to set off the whiteness of their complexion.

"I cannot conceive," I once said to one of them, "how you contrive to place your pips on the very same spot to-day as you did yesterday."—"I never take them off."—"Not to wash your face?"—"Why should I wash my face?—it is always clean."

At Warsaw, one half of the inhabitants is composed of foreigners, and especially of Germans. The Polish Jews carry on all, or nearly all, the traffic; they are innkeepers, shopkeepers, tailors, shoemakers; the Germans are physicians, surgeons, apothecaries, lawyers; the Poles, properly so called, are either nobles or peasants, either slaves or great landed proprietors: in this country there exists no intermediate class.

Society at Warsaw closely resembles that in Paris. The ladies there are extremely amiable, and they are not in any respect behind our charming countrywomen. They follow the French fashions, and affect the manners of Paris. The Poles speak nothing but French, even in conversing with one another; it is thought extremely vulgar in Warsaw to speak Polish, unless when you are talking to your servants. The Polish language is banished from good company, as the *patois* of Provence is at Marseilles. The study of foreign languages serves as the ground-work to the education of the Poles of both sexes. It is very right of them to learn the languages of other nations; for nobody, I think, would be induced to learn theirs. I certainly did make the attempt; but how is it possible to acquire the pronunciation of words, in which you find four or five consecutive consonants!

A hackney-coach horse, at Paris, is not quite so miserable as a Polish peasant, who toils all the year round for the profit of his lord. The country is fertile in corn, yet the peasant never tastes bread. Potatoes, milk, and millet, constitute his food. These people are always clothed in sheep-skins, with the wool inside in winter, and outside in summer. Their excessive filthiness engenders not only hosts of vermin which devour them, but also a disease, known, I believe, only in Poland and Russia. When a person is attacked with this disease, called the plica, his hair is clotted and twisted together, and looks like the serpents of the Euminides, and blood oozes from it if it be cut: there is no cure for the complaint, and the patient expires in frightful convulsions. Nothing can convey an idea of the nastiness of the Polish villages. No peasant in Poland ever thinks of sweeping before his door. In the cantonments occupied by the French army, the inhabitants were obliged to sweep the streets, and a greater vexation could not be inflicted upon them. These filthy, indolent clowns, nevertheless, make very cleanly and also very brave soldiers. In their peasants' dress they have a dull, stupid, brutish look; but when they have put on the uniform, and been sharpened up at the regiment, you would not know them again. These brutes become proud, cleanly, intelligent men, and are not in any respect behind the soldiers of the most civilized nations.

The Polish horses are small; they are harnessed four abreast; they are excellent animals, and very swift: they will eat anything that is given to them, even the old straw which has served to thatch houses. They were not affected by the privations incident to war, while our fine Norman horses were reduced to skeletons if they went without oats for a fortnight. The carriages of the gentry are usually drawn by four or six horses, two abreast. The traces are of immoderate length. At Warsaw, a carriage and four occupies more space than, in Paris, that of the king, with eight horses before it. This is a pompous way of moving about, and for that reason it is that it has been adopted by the Poles: they are fond of ostentatious display, of whatever has an air of magnificence. Their servants are covered with gold lace—false gold, it is true—but, at a distance, it makes a show. It is in winter that the Poles exhibit the greatest extravagance in their equipages. You then see sledges of all shapes; the horses covered with bells, and the servants with furs, present a singular sight. In summer, the north of Europe resembles our southern provinces; but in winter it has a particular physiognomy, which is exclusively its own.

I had established my head-quarters of sub-lieutenant at the mansion of Kludzienko, five leagues from Warsaw, the owner of which had forsaken it. I was its lord and master. The account of a little adventure which befel me there will serve better than all I could say to prove the excessive misery of the Polish peasants. I was alone in my chamber; the soldier who lodged me slept in an adjoining room. One night I was awakened by the creaking of my door, which some one opened with caution, and I saw, by the light of my fire which was nearly out, the bearded face of a peasant belonging to the household, who used to cut up the wood that I burned for fuel. He looked about, and as I pretended to be asleep, he entered. Not knowing with what intention this man had come to my chamber at such an hour, I gently stretched out my hand, grasped my sword which was near the bed, and prepared to run him through the body if I perceived any hostile demonstration: but the poor devil had not the least notion of attempting my life; a parcel of candles was the aim of his nocturnal expedition. I had hung it up near the fire-place; thither the robber directed his course; he seized the candles, retired, and shut the door. If the candles had been unfortunately placed near my bed, I should have concluded that the intruder had come to murder me, and most likely have killed him.

Astonished at his running this risk for such a trifle, I was curious to ascertain what he would do with my candles; for in Poland, and even in many German villages, the peasants light themselves at night by means of pine splinters, which they burn one after another; and I could not suppose that my man coveted such a luxury for the purpose of lighting his smoky cabin. I dressed myself forthwith, and, knowing his house, I ran thither. Through a wretched casement I could see them engaged in frying my candles with potatoes; the poor fellow's whole family was impatiently awaiting the moment for partaking of so savoury a dish; they watched with looks of delight all the details of the culinary operation, and presently all of them eagerly joined in devouring the delicate mess. I returned home with my head full of philosophical reflections, and the peasant never was aware that I knew the thief who had stolen my candles.

In pleasures, with a single exception, there is nothing positive in this world: every gratification is relative to the position of the individual; and the more severe have been the privations, the greater is the pleasure. Hence it was that with the persons saved from the wreck of La Meduse, a drop of liquid dentifrice composed of alcohol was an inestimable favour, which each was anxious to obtain in his turn. My candle-eater, who had never swallowed potatoes cooked in any other way than simply boiled in water, made of them when fried brown in tallow a most delicious meal, as good, nay, perhaps better, than Verey's and Beauvilliers' dinners are to the dilettanti, long habituated to the scientific combinations of transcendental gastronomy. The Cossacks, accustomed to plum-wine, and to the stinking fermented sap of the birch-tree, preferred brandy saturated with pepper to our best Burgundy, which imparted but obtuse sensations to their horn-cased throats.

Some time afterwards, my lucky star caused me to be quartered at Kozerky, the seat of Count Lesseur, formerly chamberlain to the last king of Poland, whose kind hospitality I shall ever hold in the most grateful remembrance. M. Lesseur was of French extraction; he had held high appointments at the court of Stanislaus, and, since the partition of Poland, he led the life of a philosopher with his wife and Mademoiselle Annette, his most virtuous and amiable daughter. This worthy family combined the information, the talents, and the urbanity, of civilized life with the simplicity of the patriarchal manners. I shall give a description of the mansion of Kozerky, that the reader may be able to form some idea of what is called a mansion in Poland. Some rich nobles certainly have finer seats, but the number of those who live in worse habitations is infinitely greater: I therefore take that of Kozerky as the average medium.

At the end of a long line of huts, cabins, kennels if you please, called houses, and serving as stables and lodgings for peasants and their horses, you perceive a small, neat, nay, superb-looking house, because the points of comparison beside it are all to its advantage. It has only a ground-floor, raised a couple of steps, and attics above: the door opens upon a corridor, which runs from one end to the other. In this corridor are seen four doors; on the right is the dining-room, on the left the drawing-room, beyond are two bed-chambers, and that is all. Each apartment, floored with deal, and neatly furnished, is provided with an enormous stove, heated from without. The windows have double-glazed sashes, to keep out the cold: between the two are kept flowers, and sometimes birds. The whole house is thatched, and, among the generality of the country nobles, it differs only in the greater or less number of rooms in proportion to that of the inhabitants. The kitchen, the servants, the horses, are in a neighbouring building: there the steward lives, but he eats at his master's table, and, as I have observed, drinks out of the same glass with the family. This steward is almost always an educated man; I have seen many a one who spoke Latin extremely well, but, from the manner in which it is pronounced in Poland, the professors of our university would not understand a word of it. In Latin, as all who have learned that language well know, you *thou* everybody; but, in Poland, the habit of servile expressions has introduced a phrase which was not known to Virgil and Cicero. Instead of saying *tu* (thou), the Poles say *domioniat tua* (thy lordship), and this periphrasis occurs incessantly in their conversation, requiring perpetual agreement in gender, number, and case, in a most perplexing manner. A peasant is always bent down to the ground when he speaks to his lord, or to any man dressed otherwise than in sheepskin. Every time he opens his mouth, he extends his right-hand and bows his head to touch the feet of the person facing him; which made our soldiers say, when a peasant desired to speak to us: " Lieutenant, here is a man who wants to measure you for gaiters."

Were you to see a Polish gentleman travelling and in his mansion, you would not believe that it is the same person. At home he lives upon salted meat, cabbage, and paste-balls; he drinks nothing but wretched beer and still more detestable brandy. When he travels, it is in his carriage drawn by four or six horses, escorted by a party of moustached lacqueys, beplastered with lace, and champagne is his only beverage. At such times nothing is too costly, for the essential point is to cut a figure: if he has not money, he borrows; the Jews are always ready, and God knows at what interest they furnish it. For no consideration in the world would a Polish noble renounce his journey to Warsaw at a certain time of the year, and still less the entertainment which he annually gives there; because his ancestors did so, he must do so; and were he to miss, he would think that he was disgracing his most remote posterity. There is a striking resemblance between the French character and that of the Poles. Like them, we are fond of display: like us, they are brave, as they have proved thousands and thousands of times.

When a Pole travels in winter, he always has a sledge upon the imperial of his carriage. If snow falls, the carriage is set upon the sledge; if it thaws, the sledge is lifted upon the carriage. In this manner the journey never suffers any interruption. The traveller must take his bed with him, if he wishes to lie on something better than straw; he must also have with him provisions of all kinds, if he would make sure of dining every day. The master's carriage is followed by one or more carts, filled with baggage and servants; it is a real caravan. In all the villages you find a *Jew's house:* this is the inn, and, good heavens! what an inn! Go in, ask for anything but beer, wretched brandy, half-baked paste, which they call bread, and the invariable answer will be—*Niema* (we have none). In Poland, this is the answer to everything, excepting when you ask for water; in this case, they say *Zara* (directly). You should see what nastiness pervades these abodes of the children of Israel. One day, when I was quartered at one of these inns, I perceived that dirty sheets had been put upon my bed. I sent for the landlord, and begged that he would have them changed. "And why so?" he asked.—"Because they are not clean." —"You are quite mistaken; they have only been slept in by three or four French officers." I could not make this son of Jacob comprehend that sheets may be dirty before they are quite black.

The Jews of Poland are a distinct people; they certainly resemble the Jews of other countries, inasmuch as they are incessantly striving to make money; but they differ from them in not spending any. They heap dollars upon dollars, and they are content, though frequently beaten. In France, in Germany, a rich Jew lives like a rich Christian; but, in Poland, he goes about in the garb of a pauper; and if, deceived by appearances, you offer him a couple of sous, he will not refuse them.

In Poland, the roads are neither firm nor paved: no farther trouble has been taken than to cut them through the forests—that is all. In winter, and when the French army was traversing the country in all directions, we met with oceans of mud, which it was impossible to cross. The mud of Pultusk has acquired unlucky celebrity; horse-soldiers were smothered in it, together with their horses: others blew out their brains, despairing of ever being able to extricate themselves from it.

The mention of the mud of Pultusk reminds me of the melancholy adventure of an officer of engineers. He had sunk in a slough up to his chin, and could not extricate himself. A grenadier came up. "Comrade," cried the officer, "come and help me; I shall soon be smothered by the mud."—"And who are you?"—"An officer of the engineers."—"Ah! one of those fellows who make problems! Well, draw your plan." And the grenadier went his way. The soldiers disliked the officers of the engineers, because they never saw them fight with the bayonet. They could not conceive how it was possible to render services to the army with a pencil and a pair of compasses; and were like Laborie, who did not think that Malte-Brun could be a good geographer because he was not on the field of battle of Eylau.

When the roads become so bad as to be absolutely impassable, then, and not till then, are repairs thought of. Logs, cut to the same length, are then laid across the road, close to one another. If you wish for a sound shaking, just trot over one of those roads. These singular pavements are of unequal width; no pains are ever taken to cover them, and Heaven knows how you are jolted. Roads, thus repaired, are very dangerous for the horses; for it frequently happens that two pieces of timber separate, or perhaps they break, and the animal sprains his leg. But who cares for that? horses are cheap enough. Between Warsaw and Posen, the road is frightful in winter; the villages are the filthiest that can be imagined; the only tolerable station is Lowiez, a pretty little town; but Kutno, Sempolno, Klodawa, Slupcé —what sewers!

Posen, as well as several Polish and Prussian towns is built of wood and brick: stones are very rare in that part of the country. The streets, nevertheless, are paved; and the way in which this is managed is as follows:—Every peasant, entering a town with a cart, is obliged to bring and throw down, near the gate, a stone of a certain size: those vehicles whose drivers do not pay this tax are not allowed to enter. Hence a heap of stones is seen at each gate of the city, and from these heaps are taken the materials for repairs. At first sight, it would appear easy to pay such a contribution; but persons coming every day, who have of course to bring three-hundred and sixty-five stones, are obliged to go a great way in search of them, for the environs of the towns have been, as it were, sifted through a riddle.

I have said that the Poles eat very little bread; a bit, about the size of a crown-piece, is placed for each person, and they leave half of it. The first time that I dined in a Polish mansion, the servant handed me a plate, containing a number of small pieces of bread, and I swept off the whole of the contents. I perceived a smile upon every face, and my neighbour informed me that I had taken the bread destined to serve fifteen persons. Still it was far from satisfying my appetite, for, to the great astonishment of those gentry, I was obliged to ask for more.

It is a general custom in Poland for the men, after each meal, to kiss the hands of all the ladies. When the guests are numerous, the ceremony is long, and it is curious to observe the bustle which then prevails in a spacious saloon, while the gentlemen cross one another in all directions, for each of them must kiss all hands. The ladies keep their notes *in petto,* and woe betide the wight who should fail to kiss with the requisite fervour!

Balls open with the *promenade,* in which all who are present may join : the eldest gentleman chooses a lady, and, while the music plays, he gravely walks away, taking her by the hand. As soon as he is in motion, all the gentlemen take their partners and place themselves behind him, down to urchins three years old, who are not excluded from the party. The column winds in the apartment to prolong the promenade, like the soldiers in a melodrame, who march round the stage to make their exit at the side at which they were stationed. To join in the promenade, nothing is required but a couple, male and female. When a gentleman has not been able to find a partner, he puts himself at the head of the column when it is in motion, bows, claps his hands, and makes his spurs clank from time to time by putting his heels together.* The gentleman who walks first then resigns to him the hand of his lady, turns round, claps his hands, clanks his spurs, and receives the hand of the partner of the person immediately behind him; the latter performs the same ceremony, and so on to the end of the column, where the last gentleman finds himself alone and goes and begins over again the

* In Poland, everybody wears spurs, they are never without them; they wear them when they dance, and I am not certain that they take them off when they go to bed.

same manœuvre, by dispossessing the leader of the file. In this way they proceed in general till the person who was first, having given his hand to all the ladies in succession, finds himself put out of the line; as he is always the senior of the party, he goes and sits down, and everybody follows his example.

Lovers find the promenade very agreeable, because, without exciting notice, they are sure to fall in with the lady of their choice; and everybody knows that when you take by the hand the object of your affection, you may say a great many soft things to her without uttering a word. The tune which is played to the promenade is known to everybody, it may be said to be a national air: at the very first bar, each he takes his she, and falls into the ranks. Alphonso, King of Aragon, surnamed the Magnanimous, said: "The only difference between a madman and a man who dances is that the latter is sooner out of his fit." I was always of the same opinion as that worthy monarch. I never learned the art of performing *entrechats* and *jetées battus*, or of displaying my graces in making the *queue du chat*, and yet I excelled in walking the promenade; I clapped my hands loudly enough, and I could accompany that sound with the clanking of my spurs, when I had them on.

The day after my arrival at Posen, I was quartered on the Countess Fischer, who possesses a handsome mansion in the environs. She was a tall, beautiful, and most agreeable woman. For about an hour I had been in her saloon, chatting with her, when a handsome man entered. "My husband," said she, "let me introduce you." This husband treated me with great politeness, and the conversation continued. We talked about politics, about rain, and about fine weather, when another person was ushered in, a remarkably fine man, bowing very gracefully. He grasped very cordially the hand of M. Fischer, and kissed that of his lady.

"It was very unkind of you, my friend," said she, "not

to come yesterday: we expected you to dinner, and were in an ill humour all the evening on account of your absence."

"You must be convinced, my dear countess, that reasons of the utmost importance prevented me from coming, for you know that I am nowhere so happy as here."

"We are fond of believing so," replied the husband.

"To prove it, I have to tell you that I am come to stay a week with you."

"That is delightful!" exclaimed the count and countess both at once; "that is very kind of you; nothing could gratify us more."

"Till dinner is ready, my dear friend," said M. Fischer to the last comer, "I wish to acquaint you with a plan of embellishment. Come along, let us leave the French officer for a moment alone with the countess. The character for gallantry which those gentlemen possess, and which they deserve, causes us to hope that she will not miss us." And the two friends retired, arm in arm.

The countess looked at me, striving to read in my eyes what I thought of the new comer.

"Your brother, I presume?" said I.

"No, sir."

"A relation."

"No, sir."

"Ah!"

"What means that ah?"

"Oh! nothing."

"Confess the truth; you fancy, I dare say, that this gentleman is my lover?"

"Madame...."

"No matter; I will satisfy your curiosity. Besides, why should I make a secret of what everybody knows? That gentleman was once my lover, and for three long years he was.... my husband!"

" Your husband !"

" Yes, sir."

" That is very extraordinary."

"So you may think; but it is the truth. We loved one another at twenty to distraction; it was a romantic passion, a mania, an adoration. Some obstacles opposed our marriage; our love was increased by them, if possible: at length we married. You will conclude, no doubt, that we were now happy. Our happiness lasted a fortnight at farthest: the rest of the three years that we lived together was a hell upon earth. Our tempers could not agree in anything; we were incessantly quarrelling; in short, we could not bear the sight of one another. We parted by mutual consent; a divorce was subsequently obtained, and some time afterwards I married M. Fischer. But mark the capriciousness of human nature!—the man whom I adored as a lover, whom I detested as a husband, I have now the highest esteem for as a friend. M. Fischer is fond of him, and we cannot do without him. He is a delightful friend; he is devotedly attached to us, that we are both certain of. There is no sacrifice that he would not cheerfully make, if he could be of service to us."

" I can easily imagine that your first husband regrets what he has lost. I am quite sure that in his place . . . ."

" French gallantry, all that. You are mistaken, sir. He regrets nothing."

" But in M. Fischer's place, I should be very much afraid lest . . . ."

" Lest what ?"

" Do you know our La Fontaine's tale of the *Troqueurs ?*"

" I do, sir."

" Well then, you must now know what I should be afraid of."

" That idea will never enter any of our three heads. I know that in the world people talk scandal on the subject, but that gives us very little uneasiness. We have resolved to be happy in our own way, and to adopt for our motto :— '*Honi soit qui mal y pense.*'"

EDITOR'S REMARKS

ON

CHAPTER IV.

The most striking part of the fourth chapter is that which describes the state of the unhappy Poles, by which I do not mean those brave men who have been driven from their country by the false and ferocious government of Russia, and who are obliged to seek refuge in other countries. I mean that unhappy peasantry which these very refugee nobles have reduced, by their oligarchical rule, to a state of such servitude, that they bow to the earth before every man who is not clad like themselves in sheep-skins! In short, what the Emperor Nicholas has done to the Polish nobles these did to their serfs: the consequence is, that the nobles are in exile, the country wild, and without roads that are passable, and the labouring man thinks it a luxury to eat tallow-candles fried with potatoes, and even that he cannot have without committing a robbery. Such are the effects produced by depriving man of his rights! such are the fruits of slavery! Is it strange that a people reduced to such a state of brutality should be partitioned? I think not. The Poles are brave, but they were never free. The people fought for their tyrannical oligarchs, not for their own freedom. They fought bravely, because serfs naturally adhere to their chiefs against strangers; it was not that they loved their chiefs, but that they hated the Russians. The Poles could not have been subdued by Russia, had the people possessed any degree of freedom; but an oligarchy always is, and always must be, feeble.

However, all rational people must pity the Polish refugees. Had they been victorious, a constitutional sovereign would probably have ruled Poland, for in these days no new government can be formed upon any other than free principles: instruction pervades the poorest classes of labourers, and instructed millions will not submit to the rule of an oligarchy. A constitutional kingly government, or a self-styled republic, are the only forms of government that the press will permit: and the paramount power of the universe is the press. When Polish peasants learn to read and write, Poland will throw off the Russian yoke, or, which is the same thing as far as human happiness is concerned, make that yoke just. It is assuredly of no moment to a nation who may be its rulers, provided that the people have just laws, that is to say, laws made by their representatives: just laws amalgamate the conqueror and the conquered, or would do so, were the experiment to be tried—which it will never be; for men do not encounter the dangers attending the work of robbery for the pleasure of restoring their plunder to the owners. England begins at last to discover that a system of robbery and murder is bad policy, as well as bad morality. She now begins to find that Ireland and the East will be better markets for being well treated, and the "turn of the market" is to England both the law and the gospel.

I shall not continue these notes, because there is nothing in the remaining chapters to compare with the English troops. These chapters are admirable descriptions of military life, and do great credit to the wit and abilities of the author, who is an extremely agreeable writer, and whose style and subjects are peculiarly suited to the expressive language of his country.

CHAPTER V.

QUARTERS (CONTINUED)—SPAIN.

I HAVE now introduced to you the Germans and the Poles; since we have time, both you and I, let us take a trip to Spain. In general, when you cross a frontier, you are prepared long before-hand for the change of manners and language by insensible demi-tints. Here, the people speak French and at the same time understand German; farther on, they speak German, while they mangle French. It is not till you are ten leagues on the other side of the Rhine that you find yourself in Germany. The same is the case on the frontiers of Italy and of Poland; but once across the Bidassoa, you are in Spain, completely in Spain. Two minutes before you were in France; you are a thousand leagues from it when you are over the river: manners, language, dress, in short everything, are different. The transition from St. Jean de Luz to Irun is as great as from Calais to Dover, and yet the Bidassoa is but a rivulet.

In this singular country everything was new to me, and I passed my days in running about the streets, into the coffee-houses, into the shops, to make my observations. The Spanish language is very easy for a Provençal who understands Latin, and I could soon keep up a conversation with anybody. But the Spaniards are not talkative; instead of the gaiety, the open, frank, and straightforward manner, which characterize our nation, I met with none but care-wrinkled brows and dark scowling faces, of which the tyrants in our melodramas are admirable copies. Look at those groups at the corners of the streets, in the public places. To smoke a cigar, and to do nothing, seem to constitute supreme felicity for these people. In France, when ten persons are collected together, you cannot hear your own voice: every one wants to speak, every one seeks to shine in the conversation. In Spain, all is sullen silence. Muffled up in a dingy mantle, covering garments still more dingy, suffering nothing to be seen but half their faces and the two fingers that hold the cigar, the Spaniards remain whole hours planted one opposite to another, without speaking, and puffing clouds of smoke into each other's faces. From time to time, some one takes it into his head to open his mouth: the most loquacious of his auditors then reply *Pues*. This *pues* is a preposition, a conjunction, an interjection, that is, an answer to everything. According to the manner in which it is pronounced, according to the affirmative, dubitative, or negative movement of the head which accompanies it, this word signifies, yes, no, but, nevertheless, it may be so, you are right, I do not believe it, &c. &c.

What a difference between our quarters in Germany, and especially the good-natured faces of our hosts! Instead of the most scrupulous cleanliness, and the kindness of the people beyond the Rhine, we had to encounter the nastiness and sour looks of the Spaniards. Though accustomed to the climate of Poland, we felt cold in Spain. In Biscay and in Castile it is impossible to have a fire in winter; nobody has the least notion that a door, a window, is made to shut. A floor-cloth, a carpet, are unheard-of luxuries; the trade of chimney-sweeper is unknown, for there are no chimneys. In the kitchens you see a hole at which the smoke escapes, when it can escape at all. In large towns, such as Burgos and Valladolid, you find one or two fire-places in the houses of the great, and most of these were built by French generals, who wished to make their quarters comfortable. General Dorsenne had a fire-place erected in all the houses in which he lodged.

People everywhere warm themselves with a *brasero*, an iron vase, filled with charcoal, lighted in the morning in the street. It is placed in the principal room, where all the inmates of the house meet. There, forming a circle, they scorch their knees; thus making, it is true, due compensation for their backs, which are always chilled with cold. Men and women hand round the cigarito, which serves alternately for all, and the conversation is as animated as in the streets. The handsomest woman feels no repugnance to take the cigar that is just withdrawn from the mouth of a monk; for my part, I smoked all alone for myself, as in Poland I drank by myself out of a glass of my own.

In France, the landlord of a house lets you an apartment, a chamber; you bring your bed, you dine upon what you think fit to provide; that is nothing to him. The same is the case in the Spanish inns; you hire the place which you mean to occupy during the time that you intend to stay; it is afterwards your business to run about the town in quest of provisions, if you are hungry; and to procure a truss of straw, if you dislike sleeping on the bare boards. Next day you will be required to pay the rent of the chamber, and over and above for the noise, *el ruido*, which you made the day before. This custom certainly harmonizes with the manners of a people who never talk, to whom the least noise is an annoyance, and who answer all questions by the monosyllable *pues*.

When we were quartered at inns, as it was militarily, they never made a charge for noise: the bill would have been too long for our slender purses, for we sometimes revenged ourselves for the privations that Castilian frugality imposed upon us by singing lustily. This revenge was always sure to hit its mark.

Of all the people in the world, the Spaniard is certainly the least eater and drinker; with what a hundred tradesmen in Paris consume, you might keep a thousand Spaniards. In them this temperance is not a virtue, it is the offspring of avarice and idleness. Those gentry are dainty and greedy too, when it costs them nothing to indulge. If occasion presents itself, they will pass the day in eating tarts and confectionary, and in drinking ratafia and rosoglio. The women of the Peninsula are fond of having sweet things said to them, but they would much rather have some put into their mouths. Invite a Spaniard to dinner; let the viands be delicate, abundant, and your guest will not rise from the table till he has swallowed the elements of a smart indigestion.

That man must have had his throat lined with horn, who first introduced the custom of drinking wine kept in a goatskin. The first time I tasted it, I thought that I was poisoned; I cast up the perfidious liquor, and began to drink water. When, however, the inconvenience of abstaining altogether from wine was represented to me, I drank it in spite of myself. Man gets accustomed to everything in this world; so by degrees I contrived to swallow it without making too wry faces. The *pelieco*, the *botta*, is a tarred goat-skin, sewed together, with the hair inside; a cork, or a cock, is fitted to one of the animal's feet, and it is there that the liquor is introduced and drawn out. Differing in this respect from every other movable, the older the goat-skin the higher the price which it fetches. It is the public-houses that first begin to use them; some time afterwards these sell them to the towns-people, who subsequently dispose of them to the gentry. Consequently, in the public-houses, at the inns, you are sure to find at all times fresh-tarred wine. When the goat-skins, passing through all their transitions, have arrived at the height of their glory, the wine in them acquires a very agreeable flavour. They never use casks in Spain, because there are scarcely any high roads; and because all the other roads, excepting some which run through the kingdom from end to end, are very bad. As the transport can be effected only upon the backs of mules, the cask would be too awkward a load; and besides, it would be nearly as heavy as its contents.

With the skins of young kids they make bottles that hold

one, two, three, and even four quarts : we found them extremely convenient, and each of us was provided with his *botta,* which cut a very good figure on the pommel of the saddle, between the pistols.

The *olla* composes of itself the three dishes of Spanish repasts, to which the cigarito always performs the office of an unsubstantial dessert. Put into a pot full of water, grey peas, *garbanzos,* cabbage, a plentiful allowance of capsicum, and a little piece of bacon or butcher's meat; boil the whole sufficiently, and you will dine as all Spain dines, when it has a good dinner.

Nineteen-twentieths of the Spaniards live upon the olla. People of distinction affect, on the contrary, great luxury in eating and drinking, but it is only in cities of the first class that you meet with these privileged beings. Their kitchens are well furnished; while the inferior tradesmen and gentry have nothing but a pot for the *olla,* and a few trifling utensils, worth, altogether, the sum of half-a-crown. But, great or small, rich or poor, the Spaniards are strangers to that useful instrument derived from clock-work, which we call a spit. In the kitchens of the great, a scullion performs its office; he turns *el asador* before a rousing fire, and never leaves it till the pullet and himself are thoroughly roasted.

In the villages, go in anywhere at meal-times, and you will always find the same fare without variation. Those persons who live by themselves eat bread and raw onions; they do not take the trouble to make an *olla,* because they would be obliged to light a fire for that purpose. Articles of the first necessity are cheap; and hence, a family in Spain, possessing an income of six hundred francs (£25 sterling) lives in a relative opulence, envied by all the neighbourhood.

I was frequently reminded in Spain of a sort of drama, which I had read in my youth. The Spaniards, methought, must all have learned it by heart. This *morality,* for so it was called, was written by Nicole de la Chesnaye; it has thirty-eight dramatis personæ. Its title is: *La Condemnation des Banquets, à la Louange de Diepte et de Sobriété, pour le proufit du corps humain.* This curious piece is printed at the end of a black letter quarto, entitled: *La Nef de Santé avec le Gouvernail du corps humain.*

The author strives to prove that it is dangerous to eat too much. The *morality* concludes with the trial of Banquet and Supper. Experience is the judge. Banquet and Supper are accused of having caused the death of four persons by excessive indulgence at table. Experience sentences Banquet to be hung. Diet is the executioner. Banquet confesses, says his creed, and receives absolution. Diet puts the rope about his neck, pushes him from the top of the ladder, and poor Banquet dies. Supper is only condemned to wear leaden wristbands to prevent him from setting too many dishes on the table; and moreover, he is required, upon pain of being hanged, to keep at the distance of at least six leagues from Dinner. I recommend this *morality* to the attention of our playwrights; with a few little alterations, they might manufacture a very pretty new drama out of it.

Since I have begun to quote old books, I will subjoin a passage from one which, among many silly things, contains some very pertinent observations.* "Tell me," asks one, "what are the different degrees of content."—*Answer.* "If you would have it only for a day, get shaved; for a week, go to a wedding; for a month, buy a good horse; for six months, buy a fine house; for a year, marry a handsome wife; for two years, turn priest; for your whole life, be sober."

The Spaniard, who never reads, nevertheless practises all these precepts of sobriety. It is universally admitted that the people of the South have fewer wants than those of the North. Look at the Arabs, they live a day on a few dried figs or dates, and sometimes a handful of maize-flour. The

---

* This book, in Latin, is entitled: NUGÆ VENALES, *seu Thesaurus videndi et jocandi*, 1644; apud neminem tamen ubique.

Spaniard is a stranger to the enjoyments of luxury, and to those superfluities which with us are matters of the first necessity. The arts, agriculture, mechanics, have not advanced a step since the time of Charles V. Advanced, did I say?—they have retrograded. The inns have remained at the same point; they have retained the same physiognomy as they exhibited when the heroes of Cervantes flourished. With the most beautiful plantations of olives, the Spaniards eat detestable oil; with superb vineyards, they drink muddy wine, without conceiving the slightest wish for any improvement whatever. When I have chanced to make observations on this subject, they have replied:—"Our fathers always lived so; how can we do otherwise?"

In Spain, the comfortable is unknown, perhaps disdained; the native of the Peninsula does not set his heart on those trifles, to which we attach such value. The supply of absolute necessaries, which he always found at the door of the convent, has long instilled carelessness and indolence into his habits and manners. If he is backward at engaging in regular, continued labour, he is active enough in contraband pursuits. Among no people would you find men more robust for performing long marches, more daring for attempting hazardous enterprizes, more persevering and more obstinate in following up a scheme which they have adopted.

The wars which the Spaniards waged for ages against the Moors caused the population to collect in the towns. You rarely see hamlets scattered over the country; villas, such as we have around our towns, are absolutely unknown. This congregation of the inhabitants at certain points gives a singularly dreary aspect to the country, and renders the roads unsafe. Spain has been in all ages the country of adventurers; no other could have been the native land of Don Quixote. The numerous lines of custom-houses that intersect the Peninsula have produced smugglers. A smuggler who finds his stratagems defeated, sometimes turns highwayman : these two professions are brothers. The Spaniards, accustomed to extol the exploits of the former, have been led by an insensible progression to admire those of the latter. Thus robbers and smugglers, heroes placed upon the same line, have always been in readiness to become chiefs of the guerillas. Their troop was formed, the nucleus was there; it increased, like the snow-ball, the farther it went.

All those men who have gained an illustrious name in a corps of partisans, would, probably, have remained unknown in a regular army. Each was anxious to be thought something of; fighting under the observation of his neighbours, he was sure to be seen, praised, celebrated in extempore ballads. Every day he was repaid for his courage by the commendations of his countrymen : in a regiment, he would have been lost in the crowd, and, if he had distinguished himself, in his own village his merits would have been unknown. This fondness for celebrity was always a prominent trait in the Spanish character : for this it is that the torreador risks his life, amidst thunders of applause, which he fancies he has as richly deserved as if he had saved the country ; and for this it is that the Spaniard, when he finds no legitimate occasions for signalizing himself, turns bandit or smuggler.

No country in the world is more favourable to partisan warfare than Spain. It everywhere abounds in excellent military positions, and if, to these topographical advantages, you add the temperance of the inhabitants, you will know the secret of all the insurrections past, present, and to come. You will also know why civil wars are interminable in that country. The chiefs of all the parties have a certain importance which they would lose the very day on which peace should be signed. Every commander of troops is a sort of viceroy, who governs without control all the countries which he overruns. He makes requisitions of provisions, he levies imposts : in a state of peace, he would be reduced to his moderate and ill-paid appointments. Hence it is that the war, which is at this moment desolating Spain, lasts so long and hence, too, no one can foresee its termination.

In the time of Louis XIV., Marshal Villars was in Catalonia. One day, his nephew, who was serving as his aide-de-camp, came to him in breathless haste:—"Sir," said he, "I am come to bring you important intelligence. A corps of six thousand Spaniards is to pass a certain defile in two hours. I have received positive information to that effect. If you will despatch a regiment immediately to occupy the mountains, you may catch all those Spaniards at a single hawl of the net."

"Very well, desire breakfast to be brought."

"Yes; but shall I not first carry your orders to the colonel?"

"I tell you I want my breakfast."

"But, sir, if you let this opportunity slip, you may not have such another."

"Let us sit down to breakfast."

The marshal made a hearty breakfast without speaking a word. His aide-de-camp was dull, and could not account for his conduct. By and by, taking out his watch:—"'Tis now too late," he exclaimed; "the Spaniards have passed the defile!"

"Why should they not pass, simpleton? Certainly I could have taken them all, and put an end to the war to-day. But what would have been the consequence? I should have returned to Versailles, to be lost in the crowd, or, perhaps, to Villars, to die of *ennui*. Now, I like much better to stay here as commander-in-chief of the armies of Louis XIV."

An insurrection like that of Spain, against Napoleon, would be impossible in France for any cause whatever. Among us the meanest house-keeper possesses furniture, provisions, a certain degree of comfort; to these he is as strongly attached as to life; he would not forsake his house, for fear of finding it empty at his return. In Spain, all these things are reduced to the simplest expression : the Spaniard, for it is the man himself who undertakes the duty, buys every day the necessaries that are wanted. He goes to market for the wood, the charcoal, the wine, the bread, the oil, the salt, requisite for the day; by night all is eaten, burned, drunk: there is nothing left; the family might set off, it would have nothing to leave behind it but a few old pieces of furniture of no intrinsic value. Compared with the Spanish tradesmen the artisans of our cities possess all the luxuries of material life; they are Sybarites, real Sardanapaluses.

In Spain, people have scarcely any linen: the peasant is wrapped in a brown mantle, the citizen in a blue one, which admits of his having a dirty shirt, or even none at all; consequently they can shift their quarters at a very trifling expense. In Madrid and the large cities, you see fashionable people dressed in the French style, but these are exceptions.

All the arts owe their origin and their improvement to the necessity for eating, which is of daily recurrence among men. If there existed in nature any common and abundant food, which each could procure without labour, as there exists a beverage of which we may drink as much as we please; if this food were at the command of all, like water; we should still be in the woods, clad in the skins of beasts, and never think of building cities and constructing rail-roads. It is the necessity for eating that gives rise to all the ideas of art, science, and civilization. Rabelais calls the stomach Messire Gaster, the first master of arts in the world, and Rabelais is right. After what is necessary, men want the superfluous; from the cake baked in the embers, to the box at the Opera, there exists a long series of things, an uninterrupted chain of wants, which has its origin in the stomach.

The Spaniard has stopped half-way; when he possesses twenty-pence, he is sure of his food for a week, and will not do anything for that time. The love of gain will not overcome his hereditary indolence, that unconcern for the morrow, which raises between France and Spain a barrier loftier than the Pyrenees. The *far nada* is supreme happiness for the Spaniard, as the *far niente* for the Italian. He has not the fortitude for labour; no matter, so he has that for privations. The happiest man is he who has the fewest wants; this applies to nations as well as to individuals.

In France and elsewhere, when we have satisfied the cravings of the stomach, that is not sufficient; we want decent clothing, linen, furniture, which we renew at certain periods. The Spaniard never renews anything; his furniture, his utensils, confined to what is strictly necessary, served his grandfather, and will suffice his great-grandchildren. Over him Fashion has no influence; that divinity of the first order among us has no altar in Spain. People there dress as they did in the time of Philip V., and as they will do a hundred years hence. In every part of the kingdom, both sexes wear the same costume: at Madrid, Seville, Valentia, and Vittoria, it is the black gown and the black veil for the women, the brown or blue cloak for the men.

I never could conceive how it happens that, in our theatres, the managers of which pique themselves so much on truth in regard to costumes, they should permit the Rosinas, the Countess Almavivas, to dress in white and pink. Never was Rosina dressed in this manner; never had she any other than a black gown, trimmed with jet, a black mantilla, nothing but black, and that to set off the fairness of her complexion. To dress a Spanish woman in pink is as preposterous as to represent Manlius in the habit of the middle ages, with moustaches and a large dagger. It is singular that, in the hot climate of Spain, black should be the only colour adopted for the apparel of women. Imparting a certain severity to their persons, it forms a strange contrast with bright and wanton eyes, and a voluptuous air. The young look like nuns who have run away from their convent to seek their fortune in the world ; the old, like ancient sybils ; who lack nothing but a tripod to fall into convulsions.

A friend of mine, who was fond of good cheer, had a great aversion to pot-luck. Whenever he happened to come into a house where the inmates were just sitting down to table, and any one said to him :—" Dine with us without ceremony," he would immediately reply :—" It is impossible to-day ; I had rather come to-morrow." He hoped that on the morrow, the master, calculating on an additional guest would give the necessary instructions to his cook for providing something out of the common way. A Spaniard would never take so much trouble. If you give him an invitation, he will accept it to a certainty; and let your fare be what it will, be under no concern, he will be sure to think it excellent.

From the commencement of the war, a swarm of French restaurateurs had settled upon Spain. They had fixed themselves from stage to stage, from Irun to Seville inclusive. At their houses the best productions of the French soil were to be found; their active correspondence with the Chevets, the Corcelets, furnished the lovers of good cheer who had well-lined purses with a salutary resource for making a diversion to the *olla* of the Spaniards. These dealers in beef-steaks and cutlets charged extravagant prices for all that came out of their kitchens ; and these could only be afforded by those who in an army are accustomed to treble their pay by what they call perquisites. The generals, commissaries, store-keepers, could dine as they would have done at Very's or Beauvilliers'. After watching an action at a distance with his glass, a clerk in the victualling department would go to recruit himself to the great restaurant of Wagram, and dine by the card as at the Palais Royal. I attempted at first to imitate these high financial notables, but was soon obliged to stop short. *Non licet omnibus adre Corinthum* said a sage, who would not have been such if he had had his pockets full of money. Having no inexhaustible source to supply me with ducats, I was forced to live upon my rations; for it is mathematically demonstrated that it is impossible for a captain, whose pay amounts to two thousand francs, to give a louis every day for his dinner.

The day after my arrival at Vittoria, I went to a shoemaker's to get some repairs done to my boots. There was nobody in the shop; the master was on the opposite side of the street, smoking his cigarito. His shoulders covered with a mantle full of holes, he looked like a beggar, but a Spanish beggar, appearing rather proud than ashamed of his poverty. He came over to me, and I explained my business. "Wait a moment," said he, and immediately called his wife.

"How much money is there left in the purse?"

"Twelve *piecettas*" (fourteen francs, forty centimes.)

"Then I shan't work."

"But," said I, "twelve *piecettas* will not last for ever."

"*Quien ha visto magnana?*" (Who has seen to-morrow?) said he, turning his back on me.

I went to one of his colleagues, who, probably, not having so considerable a sum at his command, condescended to do the job for me.

The pride of the Spaniards is become proverbial. The meanest beggar in Spain deems himself as noble as the sovereign. Clothed in rags, he drapes himself like a Roman senator: if you refuse him alms, you must do it in a civil manner: and this is a ceremony which you are obliged to repeat frequently, on account of the innumerable host of beggars with which Spain swarms: it is the native land of Guzman d'Alfarache; this hero of the mendicant tribe could not have been born in any other.

The proverb, "Proud as a Spaniard," applies to all the classes of society. In no country, perhaps, is the feeling of equality so profound as in Spain; nowhere are the common people less cringing. The beggar preserves a sort of dignity. If he meets a nobleman, treating him as an equal, he asks permission to light his cigar at that of the marquis, and the marquis considers the application as a matter of course. These two men, who have been puffing volleys of smoke at one another, will, nevertheless, remain each at his post: the one will be still a beggar, the other still a marquis. For, in Spain, it is not as in other countries: everybody there is stationary. My father did so; I must do as he did.

Begging is a profession. Every church-door, every corner of a street, decorated with the image of a virgin or a saint, has its appointed beggar. It is a fund which they work and turn to account. A ruined man, who knows not what to do, buys the first saint he meets with, baptizes him St. Jago or St. Pancratio, sets him up near a post, and turns *santero*. The peasants give him alms; he prays for the dead, if he is paid for so doing; he recites before you the seven penitential Psalms, which he applies to any person whom you may name: this costs his employers about a penny. But, if you choose to bespeak Psalms of him, to be repeated in leisure moments, these are less expensive; he will sell you as many as you please at fifty per cent. under the current price. In such a bargain, as the seller delivers nothing, there is no reason to fear that he will sell to others what you have just paid him for; and, besides, it is impossible to recognize the property. The devotee who spends a real in this manner, conceives that she is expiating her old sins, as the courtesan thinks she is not seen when she has drawn the curtain before the image of the Virgin, which always adorns her boudoir.

When a servant has deserved punishment, his master administers a certain number of strokes with the flat of his sword—a punishment essentially noble. *Caya te, hombre!* "Hold thy tongue, man!" is the expression with which the Spaniard imposes silence on his child, boy or girl. Other people have children, our's are men—this is what they think. "The eldest sons of sovereigns are princes," said Napoleon; "mine shall be a king." The Spaniards are proud not only of themselves, but also of their sun, their towns, their villages. Read a proclamation, and you will find mention made of the heroic city of Madrid, of the invincible Valentia, of the glorious Seville. In the *Gradus ad Parnassum*, all nations are denominated brave, *armipotens;* the Spaniards gave this epithet to everything connected with their country, and never employ any but superlatives.

The Moors bequeathed to them these ideas of grandeur, together with the bull-fights. A king of Spain conceives that his equal cannot exist on earth. His widow is bound to continue a widow for life. No king is deemed worthy to possess her after him: the same principle even extends to his horses. A horse that a king of Spain has ridden must never be mounted by any other. The person of the queen is so sacred that no man dare touch her, even though it were to save her life. When the king is tired of a mistress, he sends her to a convent, where she is not allowed to be visited by persons of the other sex. This is paying rather dear for the signal honour of having shared the bed of a Spanish monarch. It is related that Philip IV. one night condescended to tap in person at the door of a lady belonging to his court, not doubting that he should be received with open arms; when she had ascertained who the gallant was, she called out to him from her bed: "I shall not open the door; I have no mind to be made a nun."

All the towns in Spain have a square, surmounted with piazzas. *Los arquillos* are a necessity for the inhabitants of the Peninsula. In fact, people who spend half the day opposite to one another, without thinking, without conversing —for the few words which they waft now and then to one another, along with a cloud of smoke, cannot be called conversation—such people have need of a shelter from sun and rain. Without *arquillos* what would they do in bad weather, or when the sun makes the thermometer rise to ninety or one hundred degrees? they would be obliged to stay at home, and they could not keep siesta the whole day.

In Spain everything is alike—the towns, the villages, the costumes of the men, those of the women: in short, everything looks as if cast in the same mould: and, if all the ladies are not handsome, it may be asserted that they all have a grace and a fascination which are inconceivable, and constitute what the Spaniards call *salero*—a term to which no language furnishes an equivalent, because in no other country is there to be found what it expresses in Spain. Virgil's *vera incessu partuit dea* seems to have been written expressly for the Spanish ladies. What eyes! what magic in their glance! You are almost tempted to say to them:— "Pray, do me the favour not to look at me." Add to these means of attraction an enchanting voice, which admirably accords with the finest language in the world, the noblest, and the most harmonious expressions; and, if you mean to keep your heart, you will not go to Spain. The black costume of those ladies, their robe, revealing their charming forms, is most becoming: they take good care not to imitate the French women in their perpetual change of fashions. No hat or bonnet ever covered their heads, and intercepted the fire of their eyes. The *mantilla* covers their hair with a skilfully calculated negligence: when, for a moment, it hides some of their charms, be certain that very soon a lucky chance will make you ample amends.

The wealthy, in general, have mass said at their own houses; their wives, who are extremely indolent, and do not rise till very late, frequently hear it in bed. Those who go to the churches sometimes attend ten or a dozen masses; and it may be affirmed that, during this whole time, nothing is farther from their thoughts than God. The church is the usual place for making assignations. The Spanish women are adepts in the language of the eyes and of the fan; with these two ways of expressing themselves, they have the talent to make their meaning perfectly understood. During the performance of the mass, they keep fanning themselves even in winter; and, as neither chairs nor stools are admitted into the churches, they are continually on their knees, squatting on their heels, a position far from graceful for a female.

When a Spaniard dies, he takes care to leave wherewithal to say a great number of masses for the peace of his soul. If he is in debt, so much the worse for his creditors, who cannot be paid till afterwards. This is called in Spain, *dexar sa alma heredera*—" to leave one's soul one's heir." Philip IV. directed in his will that one hundred thousand masses should be said for the peace of his soul; that, if he had no need of so large a number, the surplus should be said for his father and mother; and that, if they had no farther need of them, they should be applied to the benefit of the souls of those who had fallen in the Spanish wars. I should like to know in what way this king expected a judgment to be formed here, in this world, of the number of masses which it would be necessary to say, and the point at which the priests were to stop.

The Spaniards, and the women especially, are extremely afraid of spirits. Each of them has seen in his life, at least, half a dozen ghosts. Hence they are very careful, before they go to bed, to make a great number of signs of the cross, to prevent spectres from coming to disturb their slumbers; and this, as everybody knows, has been in all ages an infallible recipe.

Upon the whole, all the customs of this country are tinctured with a certain varnish of devotion, of mysticism, which is not to be found anywhere else; not even in Italy. If you go to a tertulia, if you enter a drawing-room, or, in short, any place where several persons are assembled, you salute them with the words: *Ave Maria purissima.* The company immediately responds in chorus: *Sin pecado concebida santissima.* Among the women, every exclamation of pleasure or pain is preceded by *Ave Maria :* the men use this invocation less frequently.

If the Spaniards are taciturn and reserved, the women are lively, sparkling, fond of chat, and clever in conversation. In general they are very ignorant; but natural intelligence, and the grace with which they utter nothings, prevent the deficiency of instruction from being perceived at once. They are thoroughly versed in the whole vocabulary of gallantry: all the phrases of love and sentiment are familiar to them. These flow from them upon occasion as from a spring; you would say that they had learned them by heart. These ladies display, with a certain self-complacency, the immense riches of their sensibility; they try incessantly to persuade you that their love is wholly aërial—that it resembles that of the sylphs—but they would be greatly disappointed were you to take them at their word. While distilling sentiment, if I may be allowed the expression, the Spanish women are fond of its necessary consequence. After soaring to the clouds, they descend with pleasure to the earth, to partake there of more positive enjoyments.

An officer of hussars was quartered at Valladolid, at the house of a lady of great beauty, whose husband, though old, was not jealous, which, by the by, is rather extaordinary, especially in a Spaniard. The hussars always have a declaration in readiness; the lady in question and her guest soon understood one another; but the difficulty was how to find an opportunity for being alone. The husband never quitted the house in the day-time; and at night, after the good old fashion, he shared the conjugal couch. What was to be done?

One evening, madame was seized with one of those indispositions which women always have at their call. Headache, nervous complaints furnish in Spain, as well as in France, excellent pretexts for being ill for a day; on the morrow the sufferer has a right to be as well as ever.

"My dear," said she to her husband, "you must sleep alone to-night: I am very unwell; I am in great pain; I should prevent you from sleeping, and that would make me still worse."

"Yes; but how will you manage not to be frightened? You know, when you are alone at night, you are always restless."

"Well, I will tell you: keep ringing your bell every now and then. When I hear it, I shall fancy that you are with me; and I promise you not to be afraid."

"I will do so—good night."

The orderly-word was passed to the captain, who stole into the chamber. But I ought first to tell you that the husband spoke French extremely well; and our hussar had lent him, among other books, La Fontaine's Tales. The Spaniard took up the volume to lull himself to sleep, and at every leaf that he turned over, he laid hold of the bell-rope and gave a lusty pull. "It is impossible," said he, reading on; "this La Fontaine is a slanderer; women never could devise such stratagems. None but Frenchmen could believe such absurdities; we Spaniards are not stupid enough for that." These reflections were interrupted by the frequent tinkling of the bell, which proved to the lady that her husband was thinking of her, but that he had no intention of coming to visit her. The chimes continued till sleep overpowered the happy Castilian.

Next morning the captain was laughing all alone in his chamber, when his hair-dresser arrived. The Figaro of Valladolid was astonished to find his customer in such good humour.

"Good morning," said he, "señor officer; you seem to be merry this morning: I congratulate you upon it. To laugh quite alone is not laughing at all: I should like to know the cause of your mirth, and then we should form a very pretty duet."

"Ah; it is nothing; no great matter, at least."

"So you may say, but it must have been something extremely droll."

"It was a dream that I had last night."

"Surely you will tell it to me."

"To what purpose?"

"To make me laugh, and then we should laugh together."

Thereupon our hussar unable to bridle his tongue any longer, related the occurrences of the night, under the guise of a dream. The headache, the separate bed, the repeated ringing of the bell, were none of them forgotten. Figaro thought the story extremely diverting, and, on leaving the officer's room, went to shave the good-natured husband. On entering, he laughed till he could scarcely stand.

"What plant have you been treading on this morning?"

"You need not ask me twice to tell you. I shall be delighted to relate the story; it will do you good, and make you laugh as heartily as I have done. Your captain has just been telling me one of his garrison adventures: he said it was a dream that he had last night; but it is impossible to dream anything so comical. He does not choose to name the masks, I guess; the hussars are sometimes discreet; and, besides, the affair may have happened in our city. Oh! if the husband did but know it! Oh! the women! the women! are they not artful jades!" After this exordium, the barber related the story, without omitting the slightest circumstance; and, when he had finished, he was extremely surprised that it had failed to excite even a smile on the countenance of his auditor.

When the Spanish women mention the devil, they make the sign of the cross on the mouth with the thumb of the right-hand; and the name of Napoleon was treated like that of the devil. I lodged at Pampeluna, in the house of a young and charming woman. I attempted to flutter around her, but was always repulsed. Whenever I met my pretty hostess and would have enacted the gallant with her, she drew back, as far as possible, shrunk into a corner, trembling with fear, and there, moving the thumb of her right hand, with extreme celerity, made thousands of signs of the cross, to prevent the devil, who, no doubt, was in me, from sallying forth with my words and taking possession of her. Though persevering as he is mischievous, I declare that this time he was completely foiled. Too vigilant guard was kept: a sign of the cross always made him turn tail; and devil though one be, one cannot cope with such means of defence.

And all this because I was a soldier of Napoleon's! to a certainty the executioner, returning from the performance of his office, could not have excited greater horror than I did. At first, out of self-love, I strove very hard to inspire her with more favourable sentiments, but was soon obliged to desist from the attempt, for she was ready to faint whenever I wanted to detain her for a moment to make her listen to me. Long did the thought of Señora Juana de Artieda haunt my mind in a disagreeable manner. One may console one's self for being indifferent to a woman, whose love one would wish to gain, or when forsaken by her for another; but to inspire horror is an idea with which I never could familiarize myself.

CHAPTER VI.

A DAY OF BATTLE.

When the Romans of old fought battles, the hostile armies frequently agreed to meet in a plain; each general arrayed his troops, and then, on a given signal, clouds of darts obscured the sun, and each did his best to kill his enemy without being killed by him. In the field of Fontenoy, the French and the English commenced in this manner.

" Begin, gentlemen."

" No, do you begin, if you please."

" Well, since you insist on it—present! fire !"

This procedure savoured strongly of the age of Louis XV. Red-heeled marquises, who had quitted the saloons of Versailles only the day before, could not fight like obscure plebeians. They could not dispense with elegant forms, and, nevertheless, they were not deficient in courage.

Now-a-days we no longer give a signal when we fight: begin who will, kill who can. Our generals no longer make long speeches, as generals did in Homer's time, when those gentlemen were terrible babblers. Ajax, son of Oileus, Agamemnon's general of brigade, never could command a battalion to fire without making a speech of three pages. If this is amusing for the haranguer, it is extremely tedious for the harangued.

In our days, on a day of battle, little is said, but that little is to the purpose. When the army is on the point of marching to attack the enemy, every one, from the commander-in-chief to the corporal, uses the same form of expression :—" *Sacre nom de Dieu,* forward !—forward, *sacre nom de Dieu !"* This is understood from one end of the line to the other. At Marengo, at Austerlitz, at Wagram, there was no greater expenditure of eloquence. Verily, this sort of expression produces, in certain circumstances, a much stronger effect than well-turned academic phrases. If you speak too polished a language, everybody does not understand you; while the most perfumed exquisite of them all is sure to comprehend the meaning of interjections.

Our army is in march, preceded by its advanced guard, composed of light troops. The hussars dash on like devils; they trot, they gallop, the enemy flies before them; but he soon halts; our hussars halts too. A village defended by some hundred men is in front: riflemen are sent to attack it. At the moment when our men have penetrated into the gardens, a hostile battalion comes up and makes them fall back. We send a regiment to support them, our adversaries send two; we march off ten, the enemy meets us with twenty: each brings forward his artillery; the cannons roar; presently all take part in the fray; they fight, they knock one another on the head; this cries out about his leg, that about his nose, others about nothing; and there is plenty of food for the crows and the bulletin-writers.

The science of a commander-in-chief is reduced to this — to bring up the greatest possible number of men to a given point by a certain day. Napoleon has said so, and Napoleon was a consummate judge of the matter. A general ought to know what point of the map will be seriously contested with him. It is there that the enemy will give him battle; it is, consequently, thither that he ought to bring forward his troops by twenty different routes. An order, ill expressed and ill understood, frequently causes the miscarriage of the most skilful strategic combinations, witness Grouchy's corps, which did not reach Waterloo. The first consul, before he left Paris, had, with a pin, marked on the map the plain of Marengo for the theatre of a new triumph: the event justified his calculations.

The science of the general consists farther in ascertaining the force of the enemy at such and such a point, and his weakness at such another. To accomplish this, the service of spies is indispensable. He must have clever ones, and, above all, he must pay them well. Napoleon was extremely liberal to such men; it was money well laid out. We have had generals put to the rout, because they were stingy of the funds destined for secret services.

A terrible profession is that of a spy; he is obliged to risk his life daily at cross or pile. In general, these people serve both parties: they have two passports, which they show according to circumstances. When a place is blockaded, when a corps is separated from the rest of the enemy, then not a creature is allowed to pass, and passports are unavailing; in this case a man must be a very clever spy to smuggle in any piece of information.

While the emperor was at Madrid, an aide-de-camp acquitted himself of this difficult mission with a boldness which was completely successful. Marshal . . . . . .—I really do not recollect whom—was cut off from the rest of the army by a corps of Spaniards very superior in number; the enemy's position and the nature of the ground left no hope of our being able to force it. It was important that the emperor should be made acquainted with all these circumstances, in order that a useful diversion might be effected on other points. It was impossible to pass without giving battle; and the Spaniards, masters of the heights and of the defiles, would have had too many advantages.

"Well," said the youngest of the marshal's aides-de-camp, "I will undertake to go to Madrid; I shall get there to-morrow, and I will inform the emperor of all that is passing."

"And how will you contrive to escape the gallows?"

"Leave that to me; only give me your orders."

The officer immediately repaired to a convent of monks, and went to the prior, a respectable and highly respected man, who passed for a saint all over the country, for twenty leagues round.

"Father," said he, "you must give me immediately a dress of your order: meanwhile direct the best mule in your stable to be saddled. We must both mount it and start immediately for Madrid."

"But, my son, the thing is impossible."

"No explanation."

"I cannot . . . ."

"Not another word. Here is a brace of loaded pistols;

one for you, if I am discovered, the other for myself. We shall have to pass through the Spanish army together: your habit, your character, will readily open every way to you. I shall pass for one of your brethren; if you are questioned, say whatever you please; if any one speaks to me, you must answer for me. I am ill; my tongue is paralyzed; I am going to Madrid to consult the physicians: my father is a Spanish grandee; my illustrious family is anxious that I should be cured. Find the best reasons you can to save your responsibility—that is your affair. If we are taken, you are a dead man, as well as myself: I shall then have but one thing to do, and that is to despatch you. If we succeed, as I have no doubt we shall, the marshal promises you his high protection. If we should not return, your convent will be burned to the ground."

"But, my son, only consider; at my age . . ."

"At your age, father, a man can travel on a good mule. At your age, he commands respect from all; it is for this reason that I have fixed upon you. Consider the important interests that are entrusted to you; you will be answerable to God for your own death and for my suicide."

The journey was prosperous. The Spaniards knelt down before the prior, who gave them his benediction; and they even received that of the French officer into the bargain. The travellers arrived safe and sound at Madrid. On entering the city, the aide-de-camp was recognized by his comrades, who carried him in triumph to the emperor's palace. It is scarcely necessary to add that his zeal was duly rewarded.

Sometimes, in order to avoid attacking a fortified and well-defended position, it is turned: but the enemy, anticipating this movement, places troops on the other points, and the battle instantaneously becomes general along a whole line of several leagues, as at Ratisbon. At Eckmühl, Taun, and Landshut, the armies fought on a space of fifteen leagues.

On approaching a field of battle where the combat has begun, there is nothing so disheartening to young soldiers as the language held by the wounded who are coming back from it. "Take your time," says one; "don't be in such a hurry; 'tis not worth while to run so fast to get killed."—"The enemy is ten times as numerous as we," cries another.—"They have cut off one of my paws," observes a third; "you will be lucky fellows if you don't lose both yours." To no purpose would you strive to silence them; an arm in a sling, a slash on the face, insure impunity, confer the right of insolence, and these Job's comforters continue their remarks so long as they can find any one to listen to them. You should see the faces of the conscripts on hearing such language, and especially on perceiving the first dead bodies they come to. They make a circuit of twenty paces around them for fear of touching them; presently they approach nearer; and at last they march over them without scruple.

Man gets accustomed to everything, to pain as well as to pleasure. How often have you not found that a vehement sorrow, a vehement delight, has in a fortnight become an obtuse sensation, a very ordinary matter. Recollect this at the first chagrin which befals you, and say:—"This will pass away as other troubles have done." The true philosopher, in his course through life, runs over its unpleasant accidents, and considers them as a necessary evil, like rain for instance, from which he ought to strive to screen himself. If he cannot, but must get wet through, let him hope that a fine day will come to dry his clothes. This fine day will not fail to arrive sooner or later; have patience, and you will find that I am right. But, if you meet with pleasures by the way, take care not to let them give you the slip; seize them, as it were, by the collar, hold them tight, enjoy them while they last, and catch as many of them as you can.

I have always pursued this method myself; imitate me, and you will be the better for it. For, after all, if any irreparable misfortune befals you, of what use is despair? none whatever. Fret yourself ill, dash your head against a wall; of what benefit will that be? none at all. On the contrary you will make a big bump on your brow; you will want a doctor, and doctors are rather expensive.

To prove to you the truth of my reasoning, I will relate to you a little story. You know that, after the siege of Toulon, the Republic caused all those who at that time were opposed to it to be shot. After the cannon had mowed down whole ranks, a voice cried out: " Let those who are not dead get up! the Republic pardons them!" Some unfortunate wretches whom the grape-shot had spared, seduced by this promise, raised their heads; instantly a squadron of executioners—History says a squadron of dragoons, but History must be wrong—fell upon them sword in hand, completing the slaughter which the guns had commenced. The sun soon set upon this horrible scene of carnage.

It was a fine night when one of the sufferers awoke to consciousness amid this ocean of slain: he had received ten wounds, in the head, the legs, the arms, the chest, everywhere. He rolled, he crawled, along.

" Who is there ?" cried the sentry.

" Put an end to me."

" Who are you ?"

" One of the poor creatures who have been shot. Finish me."

" I am a soldier, not an executioner."

" Put an end to me; you will render me a service; you will be doing an act of humanity."

" I am not an executioner, I tell you."

" Finish me, I beseech you: all my limbs are broken, my head is smashed; I cannot possibly recover; you will spare me excruciating sufferings. Put an end to me."

The sentry approached, and examined the state of the wounded man. In the belief that his cure was impossible, he gave way to pity. If he had fired his piece, the post would have flown to arms; he thought it better to use the bayonet, which he thrust through the body of the hapless sufferer. After all—would you believe it?—the man did not die. Next day, a grave-digger, coming to bury the corpses, found him yet living: he carried him home, took care of him, and all his wounds were healed. This man was M. de Launoy, a naval officer in the time of Louis XVI., who might certainly as well have spared himself that last thrust of the bayonet.

It must not be supposed that everybody belonging to an army is brave. I have seen men who never could get accustomed to the sound of the cannon. At Wagram, a soldier of my company fell into a violent fit of epilepsy, occasioned by the whizzing of the first ball. An officer of my regiment, after thirty years' service, had never seen fire; like the English King James I. he turned pale at the sight of a drawn sword, and he frankly confessed, " I should like much to go to the field of battle, but it is not possible; I should run away at the first musket-shot, and that would be setting a very bad example." He was, therefore, left at the depôt, where he made himself very useful in training the conscripts.

At the moment of taking the field he went back to France, and did not return till the conclusion of peace. This was a settled matter; no human power could have detained him. In war-time, he frequently brought conscripts to the army, but on the following day left it again all alone. On one occasion, however, he was obliged to stay: parties of cavalry were prowling upon our rear; it was equally dangerous to recede and to advance. Poor Ch . . had the fever; he was in a state of nervous contraction, which it is impossible to describe; and yet all was confined to marches and countermarches, without a shot being fired. One morning, in the gorges of the Tyrol, a post of ours was attacked; there was a slight fire of musketry, a fire that did not concern us, as it was a thousand paces off. Ch . . . started and ran off twenty leagues in the rear without stopping: the wags of the army even said that, though a heavy corpulent man, he leaped two ditches fifteen feet wide. It was a long time before we heard of him again; we concluded that he was either a prisoner of war or dead, but we subsequently received intelligence of his arrival at the depôt of Antwerp.

People rallied him a great deal, and he took their jokes in good part, nay, he even joined in the laugh against himself, and whenever a coward was talked of, he would say: "He is just such another as I am." He would thereupon relate what a fright he had had, how he had leaped the two ditches, and all the particulars of his journey from the Tyrol to Antwerp. He confessed so ingenuously that with him fear was an incurable complaint, that nobody liked him the less on that account. How many, not more brave than he, nevertheless talked every moment of knocking on the head and of cleaving in two; while others made a practice of getting themselves taken prisoners of war in the first skirmish, that they might be delivered at once from the dangers of the campaign; and others, again, wounded themselves, slightly it is true, in order to have a pretext for retiring till the conclusion of peace. Then they were seen returning : by their account, they had a right to all the rewards, and yet you would have needed a microscope to perceive the honourable scars of those pretended wounds. These instances were, however, rare, though some of them might be mentioned in every regiment.

If everybody belonging to the army was not brave, there were men to whose courage nothing can be compared, and that in all ranks, in all grades, from King Murat to the private fusilier, from General Dorsenne to the drummer. I could fill a dozen volumes with anecdotes of the almost fabulous bravery of our warriors. I shall relate but one, witnessed by the whole 3rd *corps d'armée* in Spain.

General Suchet had just taken Mont Olivo, in spite of the predictions of the Spaniards. "The ditches of Mont Olivo," said they, "will bury all Suchet's troops, and the ditches of Tarragona all the armies of Bonaparte." He met a wounded soldier, whom his comrades were carrying to the surgeons. "Victory! victory!" he shouted, "Olivo is taken."

"Are you severely wounded?"

"No, general, but unfortunately so much as to be obliged to leave my rank."

"Well answered, my friend; what do you wish for as a reward for your services?"

"To mount first to the assault when you take Tarragona."

"Better and better."

"Do you promise me that I shall?"

"Yes."

On the 30th of June, 1811, that is to say a month afterwards, the general-in-chief was ready for the assault. The troops were forming their columns of attack, when a voltigeur in full dress, smart as on a parade day, stepped up to Suchet. "I come," said he, "to remind you of your promise that I should lead the assault."

"What! is it you, my brave fellow! 'Tis all very well, but soldiers of your kidney are too rare for me to be prodigal of their blood. Stay with your company; by communicating to all your noble courage, you will render greater service than in getting killed by yourself."

"I wish to be the first to mount to the assault."

"You will infallibly be killed. I cannot permit you."

"General, I have your promise, and I am determined to lead to the assault."

"So much the worse, my brave fellow, so much the worse for us! Do as you will."

The columns started; our voltigeur went about twenty

paces before them; he dashed on, amidst the shower of grape-shot, was the first to mount the breach, and there fell, riddled with balls. Being picked up, by Suchet's orders, this brave soldier was carried to the hospital; a remnant of life permitted him to see, that same day, the whole corps of officers, headed by the general, who came to visit him. Suchet took off his own cross of honour to place it on the bosom of the voltigeur, who died admired by the whole army. This brave fellow's name was Bianchelli.

I shall subjoin a trait of courage of a different kind. During the civil wars in La Vendée, a republican soldier was taken prisoner and sentenced to death with all his comrades. When led out to the spot where they were to be shot, one of the Vendean chiefs, admiring the martial bearing of the grenadier, solicited his pardon of the general-in-chief.

"No pardon," he replied; "they granted none to our men, in the republican army."

"What signifies that! be you generous, and save a brave man. He is a Frenchman; he will be an additional supporter gained for our cause, and for you an attached friend, who will owe you his life."

"Well, on this consideration, I consent: if he will march with us, and cry, *Vive le roi!*"

"I promise for him.—Grenadier, come hither: I have solicited your pardon from the general; he grants it, if you will cry: *Vive le roi!*"

"*Vive la republique!*" shouted the soldier.

"Let him be shot."

The grenadier proudly returned to his comrades, some of whom were already despatched. There he stood with arms crossed and head haughtily uplifted, opposite to the muskets, when the Vendean chief threw himself at the feet of the general. "I have always served with honour," said he, "as you know; in return for the blood that I have so often spilt, I beg the unconditional pardon of this grenadier; will you refuse me?"

"Be it so; I grant it you."

"Come forward, grenadier: the general grants you life, and I hope you will not employ it against us."

" And without condition ?"

" Without condition."

" Well, then, *Vive le roi !*"

I did know, but I am ashamed to confess that I have forgotten, the name of this brave fellow. Had he lived of old, in Greece or Rome, writers and sculptors would not have failed to render him immortal.

I shall not play the part of a Bombastes, and assert here, what I have frequently heard others declare, that I never felt fear. I confess, on the contrary, that the first time a ball whizzed over my head, I saluted it with an involuntary bow; to the second I was less polite; at the third I remained firm; but, whenever I came into fire, I must own that the same forms of politeness were always exactly followed.

Yes, indeed, a man had need to be covered from head to foot with triple steel, to stand coolly amidst a shower of grape. I have often analysed the sensations experienced during the ceremony, and I confess that I was afraid. Very often the infantry plays a purely passive part in a battle; it protects the artillery, and receives the balls fired against that. It is obliged to stand motionless, to receive without returning. Ah! if the point of honour, if pride, were not there to prevent a break-up, what droll scenes would frequently occur! But each is observed by his neighbour, each wishes to have the esteem of all, and not a creature flinches. It behoves the officers, in particular, to set an example; they remain firm, and, with a loud voice, order the ranks to close.

I shall not set myself up for a hero by assuming the tone of a braggart. I shall, therefore, tell you frankly, that the finest battle I ever saw was that of Bautzen. Why so? you will ask. What was there in it more pleasing than in any other? Did the mortars, the balls, and the bullets, fall in a less dense shower ?—No; but the reason why I always thought that battle a very fine one was, because I was not in it. I was at it, to be sure, but on the top of a steeple. With a telescope in my hand, I saw everything; I judged of the passing events in a place of safety.

While they were knocking one another on the head in the plain, we were in reserve in a village; and, having nothing to do till an order should arrive to call us away, we ascended the church-steeple, and there witnessed all the exploits of our warriors. This way of being present at a battle is the most agreeable of any that I know. When you are yourself an actor you see nothing, and then . . . and then . . . and then . .

When you manœuvre, when you fire, when you are actively engaged, these qualms go off; the smoke, the thunder of the cannon, the shouts of the combatants, intoxicate every one; you have no time to think of yourself. But, when you are forced to continue fixed in your rank, without firing, and exposed, at the same time, to a shower of balls, that is by no means an agreeable situation.

There are men, however, who, endued with extraordinary strength of mind, can coolly face the greatest dangers. Murat, the bravest of the brave, always charged at the head of his cavalry, and never returned without having his sabre stained with blood. This one may easily comprehend; but an extraordinary thing, which I have seen done by General Dorsenne, and by him alone, is to stand immovable, turning his back to the enemy, facing his regiment, riddled with balls, crying, " Close your ranks !" without once looking behind him. In other circumstances I have tried to imitate him, and turned my back too; but I could not remain in that position: curiosity always obliged me to look the way from which the balls proceeded.

At the battle of Ratisbon, one of my comrades was dreadfully wounded by a cannon-ball, which hit him precisely on the muscular part on which it is customary to sit. The surgeon cut and carved and pared away not less than four or five pounds of flesh; in short, the whole was gone—the whole moon, to use the expression of the Vicomte de Jodelet. Now, before that wound, this officer was five feet high at most; after his cure he measured six. People did not know him again. He had to tell his name to all his former acquaintance; for, not only had he grown so much taller, but he had filled out in proportion. Few men are so tall and stout as he became. I give this receipt for the benefit of all those who wish to increase their stature, and I guarantee its efficacy. Besides, it is not difficult of execution; a cannon-ball, duly applied, is sure to do the job.

An army cannot march entire upon a road, with its artillery and its equipages; the head would have reached Strasburg before the tail had left the Place du Carrousel; and then, this army must be subsisted: when collected, it could not find provisions; especially as the jolly fellows who compose it usually have an enormous appetite. When you see the separate divisions drawing together, when the detached generals are rejoining the principal corps, you may confidently predict a battle. Of all those which have been fought in our time, the battle of Wagram was longest foreseen; the field was known; every one had studied it. For forty days both sides had been making, at leisure, all the arrangements for attack and defence.

The storm of the 4th of July, 1809, was, certainly, one of the most violent that ever burst over our poor little planet. It is alleged that it seconded the plans of Napoleon, by preventing the enemy from observing our movement; I can say nothing on that head; but, what I can conscientiously affirm is, that in the evening there were about fifteen officers of us together at a suttler's, where we strove to neutralize the effect of the rain by copious libations of mulled wine.

Fleuret came in: he was our eagle-bearer; he had fought bravely at Valmy, at Fleurus, at Hohenlinden, and steadily pursued the path of honour, though he frequently deviated from that marked out by grammar. We called him the S and the T box, because the worthy fellow continually transposed those two letters. He approached to partake of our bowl of wine.

"It is likely," said he, "that to-morrow there will be a great many spare caps. So much the better, for mine is not good for much, and I may take my choice. Here is one that just fits me."

So saying, he tried on that of a friend of mine, M. Guillemot, a distinguished officer, who commanded the company of artillery of my regiment.

"Have a care, Fleuret," replied Guillemot; "perhaps your cap may to-morrow be found to fit some one who has a worse."

"Impossible; it is too old."

"Then it will be picked up by some peasant, or, it may be, thrown into the same ditch as yourself."

"What do you mean?"

"I say that you, who think of inheriting the leavings of others, look very like a man who will not see the sun set to-morrow."

"Pooh! the balls and bullets know me. For these twenty years that I have been in the army, I have never yet been touched: those Imperialists are too awkward."

"The pitcher goes a long while to the well: it gets broken at last."

"To the health of him who shall be left."

"That means me, and I shall empty my glass."

Here the conversation ended. Each returned to his company and lay down. The cannon was still playing to protect the labourers, but that did not concern us, so we went to sleep. At two in the morning, Guillemot was smoking his pipe, while superintending the repair of a gun-carriage that had been damaged the preceding day, when he saw Fleuret walking all alone. He called to him.

"Up, already!" said he; "you are stirring early. We shall not cross the last arm of the Danube for a long while."

"What you said to me, last night, has prevented me from sleeping a wink. I am sure to be killed to-day."

"Pooh! an old soldier, and afraid. Fie! fie!"

"Fleuret never was afraid; he never so much as thought of danger—but, to-day, I feel that I am a dead man."

"Come, come; don't be downhearted. This battle will pass over as many others have done, and . . . ."

"Adieu."

At four in the morning, we crossed the last bridge; at ten, our division was placed in first line, and the first ball was discharged at us. It hit Fleuret on the head. This brave fellow kept his money in his cravat. It was stuffed with louis-d'ors. The ball set at liberty all these prisoners, who had not seen the light for a long time. It was horrible to see the soldiers rush upon the corpse to secure the blood-stained booty.

An officer of my acquaintance wore on his finger a superb diamond, reputed to be worth from five to six thousand francs. One day a ball carried away the arm, the hand, and the diamond. He fell, but was presently on his legs again. "And where is my diamond?" said he, running amidst the soldiers who were about to pick it up. He slipped it off the finger, and, throwing the hand to the finders, "There, my friends," said he, "I give you that; do what you please with it."

In the evening, after the victory, we were exhausted with hunger and still more with thirst. Some of our soldiers having penetrated into a house, found some Austrians drinking there, half-tipsy and making no hostile demonstration. They drank with them, and the two parties were soon on the best possible terms. Two officers of my regiment arrived.

"What are you about there?" said they to the French

soldiers. "Why are not these Austrians prisoners? Break their arms, and take these men to head-quarters."

"'Tis very kind of you, sir. What! would you have us put these good friends in prison, these brave fellows who have been treating us, these excellent Austrians, who mean us no harm?"

"I order you to obey."

"If you do not take yourself off this instant, you shall see how much we care about your orders."

The drunken fellows immediately took aim and fired at their officers. It was found necessary to send a company of grenadiers to reduce them to reason; several were killed and wounded in the brawl.

The whole French army was drunk the night after the battle of Wagram. It lay in vineyards, and in Austria the cellars are situated in the grounds upon which the wine is grown. The vintage was good, the quantity abundant, the soldiers drank immoderately; and the Austrians, had they but known that we were overcome with liquor and sleep, and made a sudden attack upon us in the night, might have put us completely to the rout. It would have been impossible to make one-tenth of the soldiers betake themselves to arms. On what threads hang the destinies of empires! All might that day have been changed; the fifth act of the great drama which had so long been performing in Europe might have had a wine-cellar for denouement. Men of genius, make your calculations; there needs but a trifle to baffle them. It is probable that the Austrians were in a similar state; for if we had drunk to celebrate the victory, they had no doubt done the same to make them forget their defeat. In the field, the great difficulty consists in knowing what state the enemy is in; a general possessing that knowledge would always be victorious.

The battle of Wagram had no great material results, that is to say, there was no great haul of the net as at Ulm, Jena, and Ratisbon; scarcely any prisoners were made; we took from the Austrians nine pieces of cannon, and we lost fourteen. When this was reported to the emperor, he very drily replied, "Take nine from fourteen, there remains five."

In general, after a battle, an order of the day acquainted us with what we had done; for we often achieved great things without knowing it. In his proclamations to the army, which Napoleon drew up himself, and the style of which was perfect, he told us sometimes that he was satisfied with us, that we had surpassed his expectations, that we had flown with the rapidity of the eagle; he then detailed our exploits, the number of soldiers, cannon, and carriages that we had taken; it was exaggerated, but it was high-sounding and had an excellent effect. After Wagram, we had not the least proclamation, not the least order of the day; nay, for upwards of three weeks we knew not the name that it was to have in history: we called it among ourselves the battle of the 5th and 6th of July; the name of Wagram we learned only from the Paris newspapers.

This battle led to the victory of Znaim, the armistice, and peace. The Austrian army effected its retreat in good order; it was beaten, but it was neither cut off nor demoralized, as on other occasions. Thus, for instance, the battle of Ratisbon had carried us on to the walls of Vienna, and that of Wagram led us no farther than Znaim, that is to say, four days' march. There we were to begin again, and we did begin again.

In the evening, the whole Austrian army was enclosed. We perceived the fires of its bivouacs within a vast circle formed by ours. We anticipated some general and decisive engagement for the following day, when it was rumoured that an armistice was signed, and that peace was about to be made. Great was our astonishment on hearing these tidings. Why did not the emperor crush his enemies when so fair an opportunity offered? Why did he consent to cease hostilities in a spot which must have been either a vast trap or a tomb for the Austrian army? Such were the reflections that occurred to every mind.

When, at a later period, the marriage of Napoleon was talked of, each reverted to the events at Znaim, and the whole army concluded that the hand of the archduchess had been the express, secret, and *sine qua non* condition of that suspension of arms. But, it may be objected, his divorce from Josephine was not only not consummated, but there was yet no question concerning it. Granted: but was Napoleon accustomed to communicate all his plans? His marriage was not talked of till after Austria was evacuated by the French army; he wished not to have the appearance of conquering an empress by force of arms. The demand was subsequently made in the regular way; it was complied with; we considered all this as a comedy, in which each performed the part previously agreed upon. But, you may again reply, in all the diplomatic notes there is to be found nothing that tends to confirm such an assertion. It is very possible, I admit, that nothing was ever written on the subject; the pride of the two emperors would have been compromised. A man no more chooses to have it believed that he takes by force the woman whom he marries, than to appear compelled to give his daughter to a son-in-law whom he detests. Perhaps the whole affair was concluded by means of a promise given at the bivouac. Be this as it may, it was generally believed in the army that the hand of the archduchess Maria Louisa was bestowed on the 11th of July, 1809.

In stating the report which was then current, I pretend not to affirm anything: in the obscure position in which I have always been, one does not see much. What I certify as true is, that officers, soldiers, everybody, believed what I have here ventured to relate. My reader may take it for a truth, worthy to figure in history or for camp gossip, just as he pleases.

A-propos of gossip—I have read in many books written during the Restoration, that there existed in the army secret societies formed to overthrow Napoleon and to re-establish the republic. It has been asserted that the society of the *Philadelphes* numbered among its members a great quantity of officers of all ranks; that its principal head was Oudet, colonel of the 9th of the line; that in the evening of the battle of Wagram he was assassinated in an ambuscade, with twenty-two of his officers. Is it possible to invent such tales, and to hope, when one publishes them, to be believed on one's word? To no purpose have I ransacked my memory, which nevertheless is tolerably faithful; I can find nothing that has the least resemblance to this story. I have questioned many of the officers who were at Wagram; none of them ever heard a word of this melo-dramatic scene; and certainly such an event would have made some noise in the army. A colonel and twenty-two officers of a regiment cannot be shot *incognito*. The *Contemporaine*, in her Memoirs, has also a good deal to say about Oudet; she does not relate his death in the same manner, but her account too is mixed up with the marvellous. She makes mention also of the *Philadelphes*, whose name was unknown till the *Histoire des Sociétés secrètes* made its appearance. Oudet was a brave officer, who died at Wagram by the enemy's fire, as every soldier must wish to die, on the field of battle, doing his duty, and not in an infamous ambuscade. He was colonel of the 17th regiment of the line, and not of the 9th; he was struck by a ball, which entered his chest and came out at his left shoulder, and this ball, to a certainty was not French. The officers of his regiment erected a monument to him at Vienna. Would they have dared to do so, if he had been shot by order of the emperor?

It is not enough for a general to possess talent; he must also be lucky. In war, circumstances combine in so many different ways, that something unforeseen is constantly occurring. When any fresh man was proposed to Cardinal Richelieu for a military appointment, the wily statesman always inquired if he was lucky, and if the reply was affirmative, the appointment was conferred. Napoleon believed in his star, though he possessed an astonishing genius—this was modesty. How many epochs were there in his life, when he was favoured by chance and by the stupidity of his enemies! At Essling, for instance, the Austrians broke down our bridges by launching against them barges laden with stones: the blame of all this mischief was laid on a sudden swelling of the Danube: the poor Danube could not contradict the report. Our bridges being broken down, the army was cut in two. If the enemy, taking advantage of our situation, had dashed headlong upon us, I am convinced that our situation would have been much more critical; our ammunition was exhausted; we only fired from time to time to keep up appearances; we had our bayonets left, it is true, but human efforts have their limits. Luckily, the Austrians knew not that our bridges were broken, though they had done all that lay in their power to destroy them. In this case, why not ascertain whether the purpose was accomplished? Most assuredly, if we had been in their place, and they in ours, the whole hostile army would have laid down its arms. In Russia great numbers of the French perished; but, reverse the parts, and not a soldier would have returned to his own country.

It is certain that great men never like to admit themselves to be in the wrong. The " sudden rise" of the Danube, the " premature winter" of Russia, furnished an excuse for want of forethought. In Russia, a winter that begins in November is not premature. It was not expected till the 1st of December, when the frost generally sets in. But who would reckon thus with the almanac! In Paris itself it frequently freezes at the same period. Besides, it was not the cold that destroyed the army; it was the want of provisions. If the soldier had been supplied with bread, if he had had a slice of beef and a glass of brandy in his inside, he would have defied the cold. As sovereigns never fail to place to the account of their vast genius what is very often but the effect of chance, it would be but fair of them to avow their faults when they commit any.

Most certainly, in the army chance must be accounted something; it is like a lucky stroke at billiards, like several partridges killed out of a covey by firing without taking aim. Nay, it is equally certain, that chance frequently baffles the calculations of the most profound diplomatists. When Frederick I., King of Prussia, was still but Elector of Brandenburg, he directed M. Bartholdi, his ambassador at Vienna, to negociate with the emperor, in order to obtain permission to assume the title of king. He was charged most especially to avoid Father Wolf, the Emperor Leopold's confessor. The instructions were in cipher. The copyist made a mistake; instead of the word *avoid*, he put *employ*. Accordingly, the ambassador addressed himself to Father Wolf, who was not a little astonished. "I have always been strongly opposed to this," said he, " but I cannot withstand the mark of confidence which the Elector confers on me; he shall not repent the application which you have made to me." The Elector gained his point. But for the mistake of the copyist, he would, probably, have been disappointed.

How many generals have become illustrious through the stupidity of their adversaries! An aide-de-camp is sent to carry an order; his horse is killed, the rider wounded; he does not arrive in time; the general is beaten: owing to this accident alone, the conqueror becomes a man of genius. Causes still more trivial may produce equally important results. Sometimes, by a caprice of chance, an army does all that it ought to do to be beaten; this is like a bully plunging his sword into his own bosom.

We were in camp, near Ratzeburg, in Holstein. The

enemy was two leagues from us. We were not fighting, or at any rate, fighting but little, merely to show from time to time that we were there. Each general well knew that it was not for him to decide the question : everything depended on what should befal the grand army, which was then at Leipzig.

One day, Marshal Davoust resolved to make a general reconnoissance to force the enemy to take arms, that he might ascertain what number of men were opposed to us. A formidable column started one fine morning, and in two hours we found ourselves before the camp of the Russians, Prussians, and Swedes; for it was composed of those three nations. The camp appeared to us to be uninhabited. Fearing an ambuscade, we advanced with caution: scouts were sent forward; they went through all the hovels, and found not a creature. What is become of the enemy? Till an answer could be obtained to this question, orders were given to set fire to the camp. In a moment, all those straw huts were transformed into a heap of ashes.

While we were looking at this immense bonfire, and each was forming his conjectures concerning the disappearance of the enemy, the cannon thundered behind us; the noise increased, and everything proved to us that our camp was attacked. "We are cut off," said the soldiers; "the Russians must have been aware of our movement; they allowed us to make it; they are taking possession of our camp, and then they will easily settle our business."

The French soldiers readily give way to panic. Four hussars on their rear disturb them more than a thousand in front of them. "We are cut off!" they always cried in such a case; and you would have great difficulty to prove to them that, if anybody were cut off, it must be the four hussars. But, in the position in which we then found ourselves, the surmises of the soldiers appeared to be correct, and their fears well founded. The Russians, apprized of our movement, had, no doubt, suffered us to pass; they had taken advantage of our absence to crush our comrades. All hesitation was impossible; we must fly to their support, we must, above all, take possession of certain heights, where three hundred men might cut off all communication between us and the rest of our troops.

We set out, and proceeded nearly on the run to the defile of Gross Mulsahn; not a creature did we meet with. We then began to see clearly that the enemy must necessarily be ignorant of our march, since he had not secured so important a position. For the same reason that we were not acquainted with his movement an hour before, he could not be acquainted with ours. These conjectures were changed to certainty, when, on approaching our camp, we saw it attacked on all sides.

Chance had caused the two hostile generals to conceive the same idea, on the same day, and in the same hour. Each meant to attack the other, and each had taken a different route. General Walmoden, who commanded the allies, was extremely astonished to see our column coming up on the rear of his troops; it was a considerable time before he was convinced that it was we; he gave us credit for a scientific manœuvre, and issued immediate orders for retreat. All his riflemen were taken, and laid down their arms. It was high time for us to arrive; for our camp, weakened by the departure of our column, was not strong enough to sustain the conflict. Had General Walmoden known how small a number of troops was left, he would certainly have made a more vigorous effort, and the consequences would have been disastrous for us. But we arrived in time, and all was saved.

A circumstance nearly similar occurred at Wittenberg. The same night and at the same hour, the besiegers and the besieged armed themselves, the former to attempt an assault, the latter to make a sortie. The two parties met full butt;

a fire of musketry was kept up for a few minutes. Each concluded that he had fallen into an ambuscade, and both ran off in the utmost confusion.

The emperor was fond of conferring promotions and decorations. After a battle, he reviewed the troops, distributing ribbons and epaulets: each hoped for something: but, after a petty affair, in which two or three hundred men were engaged, whatever might be the result, the small fry of officers and the soldiers had no room for hope. The commanding officer had taken care to draw up a superb report, sprinkled with glory, intrepidity, skilful manœuvres; and, if any reward afterwards arrived, it was always for him.

I shall here give some idea of the manner in which history was then written. In the campaign of 1813, we had an affair of advanced posts at Sprottau, a little town in Saxony. The Russian rear-guard defended itself for a moment; and on either side three or four companies of riflemen were engaged. The enemy retired, leaving in our hands a few prisoners and some baggage-waggons. An hour afterwards, we were walking in the market-place of Sprottau, talking over our morning's exploits.

"There is food for the bulletin-writers!" said an officer. "You will see by and by that we have done superb, magnificent things."

"I don't know that we have done much," said another; "but I'll be bound a great deal will be made of it."

"We shall be told that the general has gathered loads of laurels, but our regiment will not be mentioned."

"I dare say we shall have a line, and he a page."

"No mention will be made of anybody; the thing is not worth it."

"You will see, when the Paris newspapers arrive. But that we may be the better judges of their accuracy, let us immediately commit to writing the brilliant results of the day, lest we should forget them. Here are the prisoners; let us count them; sixty-four, besides three baggage-waggons drawn by twelve horses, one piece of cannon, and one artillery waggon."

A fortnight afterwards the papers arrived. Heavens! what glorious exploits we had performed!—when I say we, I mean General S . . . . With unexampled intrepidity, and by means of the most skilful manœuvres, he had surrounded, attacked, thrown heels over head, taken, killed, all that came in his way. Three hundred slain, one thousand wounded, two thousand prisoners, ten pieces of cannon, sixty baggage-waggons, were the glorious results of his strategical skill and his noble valour. He had done all this alone; our regiment was not even mentioned.

Had the general said that with such or such a regiment he had performed these brilliant achievements, everybody would have thought this perfectly natural, and the honour would have been divided: but when he wrote that, "giving way to his natural impetuosity, with a small part of his advanced guard, he had overthrown the enemy, who, of course owed his safety solely to the swiftness of his heels," the glory belonged to him alone. This part of the advanced guard is an ideal, fantastic being, whom it is impossible to personify. It is, perhaps, four men, and, as the general accomplished so much with such a force, what a fierce blade he must be! Ah! how many heroes of the same stamp could I mention, if I durst!

Virgil's *sic vos non vobis* was daily exemplified in the army. In everything, ingenuity was required for getting forward. At the battle of Eylau, a conscript brought to his captain a Russian pair of colours, which he had found in the snow among a heap of slain. "You stupid fellow!" said he, "do you take this for colours? why, 'tis nothing but the flag of a company, of no value whatever. I find such as this every day, but should never think of stooping to pick them up."

A quarter of an hour afterwards the captain was haranguing the marshal. "There," said he, "is a pair of colours, which I have taken from the Russians; it was defended by four men; they are all slain." Next day the captain was *chef de bataillon*.

The word *promotion* takes possession of every military brain at the moment of entering the service, and never quits it till the moment of retiring from the army. It is somewhat like the word *husband* with a young female. She thinks of it every day. "We are going this evening to the ball; I shall, perhaps, find a husband there." So says the one. "We are going to take the field; there will be promotion," says the other. This idea engrosses every individual in the army, from the drummer to the marshal. When we dictated laws to Europe, our generals dreamt every night that the deputies of some neighbouring kingdom came to offer them a crown of gold on a cushion of velvet.

The example of Bernadotte turned all heads: we all fancied that we had a sceptre in the sheath of our sword. A soldier had become a king; each of us thought that he might do the same. Certainly, if, from the beginning of the world, there existed a single example of a man who had not died, we should all believe ourselves destined to form the second exception to the general rule; each individual would be impressed with the internal conviction that he was immortal.

A great deal is said now-a-days about military promotion at the time of the empire, and about the gratitude of the soldiers to the emperor. The term gratitude is truly comical. What a strange abuse of words! In point of fact, did we owe any especial gratitude to his imperial and royal majesty, when he was pleased to bestow the appointments of the dead upon those who survived? And very often he who had won was not permitted to touch the stakes. After every battle, a swarm of officers sent from Paris pounced upon our regiment, to seize the best places that were vacant. The new nobility was as greedy as the old. Had the empire lasted ten years longer, it would have been mentioned as a remarkable circumstance that a commoner had been promoted to a colonelcy. We were on the point of seeing the highest plebeian ambitions grow old in the obscure honours of the rank of major. The sons of marshals, generals, counts, barons, councillors of state, and prefects, acquired a new rank every fortnight: it was by promoting them in the army for what they had not done, that the emperor encouraged their fathers.

Not that the marshals and generals were deficient in courage: they have proved the contrary on a thousand occasions; but they began to be tired of the profession. When a man possesses a fine mansion in Paris, and a beautiful country-seat in the environs, it is not agreeable to waste his life in the smoke of a bivouac. For ten years, twenty years, one might endure it—but for ever!

It was necessary to dazzle the prefects; it was necessary to render them deaf to the lamentations of mothers, to the voice of conscience, that they might send to the army all who were able to carry a musket. A general said to his soldiers who fled before the enemy: "Idiots, do what you will, you must get promotion; if not to-day, it will come to-morrow." Napoleon seemed to hold the same language to us; but you will say, under him people grew rich. Who grew rich? A superior officer, here and there; but what did the immense majority bring back? Old clothes and glory. Glory! what is glory? A bulletin in which you are mentioned. Who were mentioned after every battle? Ten persons out of three hundred thousand. And yet, every one did his duty; but it was impossible to mention everybody.

I hear it repeated every day that men went to the army to serve the country, to serve the emperor. They went to it, they go to it, and they will go to it so long as there shall be armies, some by compulsion, others to obtain promotion. The country, the emperor, the king—what do they mean but promotion? I except great political crises, when the passions and the social position sometimes silence personal interest. Men went to the army because they knew that such and such a one, from private soldiers, had become generals, marshals, princes, kings. "Why should not I do as they have done?" said every soldier, strapping the knapsack to his back. We had all of us the commission of marshal of France in our cartouch-box; the only difficulty was to get it out.

CHAPTER VII.

THE CAMP.

In the time of Louis XIV. and Louis XV. a camp was very often but a dramatic exhibition, given to the ladies of the court, tired of the pleasures of Versailles. The superior officers were mostly engrossed in their tents with the gossip of the saloons and billet-doux; they left the details of service to the majors and the officers who had their fortune to make. The colonels and the generals made it their business to arrive at the camp in splendid carriages, with a numerous retinue of servants and a good cook, and to keep open table. They ruined themselves in camp, but they made people talk about them. When it was requisite to pay with their persons, these gentlemen were not sparing of them: they fought like men of courage as we have done, and as we shall do again when occasion presents itself; but they had only the roses of the military profession without the thorns, for I do not give the name of thorns to cannon-balls and bagatelles of that kind.

To them the camp was a diversion, a medium for showing themselves off: they had hopes of being remarked by the king or by his mistresses: a word might be said at the *petit coucher*, and this word was worth a regiment. It is prodigious what an officer would then spend in camp in three months. Marshal de Boufflers squandered millions at the camp of Compiegne in 1698; he had couriers who brought him daily the wines of all countries, the rarest species of game, the finest fish: he had the honour to entertain Louis XIV. and the King of England, an honour which cost him very dear. In the poetic life of Versailles, the nobles only spent, they never calculated. "See my steward," said a great man, "settle with him; my business is to spend; the rest is his affair."

In those times, when the generals were tired of a month's campaign, they would agree upon a truce at the advanced posts, and each took up his quarters without apprising the minister. "When it rains, stay at home; we will not stir, it is so disagreeable to get splashed." Now-a-days, we march in all weathers, in all seasons, but the enemy does the same; if we have monster-mortars, or steam-guns, he will have them too. The chance will still be the same, for ten against ten are not more efficient than one against one.

By improving the art of destroying men, we shall perhaps gain one thing—we shall make wars more rare: each will stay quietly in his own chimney-corner, keeping his feet warm. Perhaps we shall even return to the times of the Horatii and the Curiatii; after going all round the circle, we shall arrive again at the starting point. While two or three champions settle the quarrel of their country, the rest will look on with the musket on their arm. Agriculture, commerce, manufactures, those three great levers of civilization, will no longer be obstructed in their operations by the follies of certain kings.

Now-a-days, when an army is in the field, it sleeps in bivouac; it is allowed to encamp only during armistices, or when peace is concluded. In cantonments the troops are too much scattered, it takes too much time to collect them, the soldiers cannot be sufficiently overlooked, discipline suffers. In garrison, it is rarely that regiments enough can be brought together for performing great manœuvres, whereas in camp, have as many as you please, you will always find room for them.

The evolutions of the camp are the school of the colonels and generals; it is there that they acquire the art of ploying and deploying their troops, that they learn to judge of distances and of the fit time for a charge of cavalry, and that they attain that partial precision which is frequently indispensable for great strategic movements.

As soon as there was a suspension of arms between the two armies, we formed camps by divisions. As hostilities might recommence every moment, it was necessary to be ready to assemble and to march, like a single man. There were also circumstances in which, without armistice, without any convention, the two armies, not being prepared to take the field, either owing to the season or to some other cause, formed camps till they should receive orders for attacking. Thus, in the first days of May, 1807, the grand army left the cantonments which it had taken a few days after the battle of Eylau, and formed camps in the environs of Osterode and Doringen: there it remained quiet till the 5th of June, when the Russians, tired of this inaction, attacked the first line, commanded by Marshal Ney. The campaign lasted nine days: on the 14th of June was fought the battle of Friedland, and soon afterwards we again began to form camps around Tilsit.

A camp is a town of wood and straw, sometimes of canvas,* laid out by line, with its streets, great and small, long and short; the whole kept extremely clean. A camp is a very

* At the time of the empire, the troops were strangers to tents; our armies marched so rapidly that they could not have carried with them all the requisite baggage, without impeding the celerity of their movements.

fine thing, but I maintain that a town is an infinitely preferable abode.

In general, in order to erect our camps we demolished villages. At Tilsit, every regiment had about thirty to pull to pieces; one or two were allotted to each company. We had a great quantity of *found* carts and horses, which served to remove the materials. With such means, it may easily be conceived that our camps were superb; those who have never seen them cannot form any idea of them. The hovels once constructed of uniform dimensions, every one turned his attention to decorating his own in an elegant manner, and soon orders arrived to take such a company of such a regiment as a model for this or that particular thing. The soldiers, vexed at having their work to begin again, invented new decorations, in order to give the innovators a job in their turn. With such a system there is no end to change. It may be said that a camp is never finished: so long as troops are there, they find something to do to it.

A regiment conceived the idea of cutting down several loads of firs in a neighbouring forest, and planting them in the line of the piles of arms, which produced a fine effect, because that tree keeps its green colour for a long time, even after it is cut. On the morrow, an order of the day directed the example set by this regiment to be generally followed; but the imitators, striving to outdo their model, planted a tree at each angle of each shed, which was deemed a great improvement, and in consequence an order was issued to imitate the imitators. Then, with a view to eclipse all, we marked out in front of the colours of our regiment an immense parallelogram, which was levelled and swept, to serve for a parade; and this space was bordered on each side by six rows of trees, which presented the appearance of a magnificent walk. All this was done as if by magic, for when you have two or three thousand hands at your disposal, and they fall to work cheerfully, the business is soon completed. The other corps soon received orders to take pattern from us; but the neighbouring woods no longer existed. War, you see, is a very fine thing; but floods, hail, fire, are less destructive than an enemy's army: France has, in her turn, had some experience of this.

The two emperors and the King of Prussia came to see our camp, and we executed grand evolutions in their presence. General Mouton, afterwards Count of Lobau, Napoleon's aide-de-camp, commanded in chief. We filed away before the three sovereigns, and before an army of princes, marshals, and generals, of the three nations. Never, I verily believe, was a greater quantity of embroidered dresses collected together upon any point of the globe. Napoleon in his simple uniform of horse-chasseur, was the ruling spirit of this multitude. Alexander and Frederick William galloping behind him, did not allow their horses to keep pace with his. They subsequently made Napoleon pay dearly for the glory with which he crushed them at Tilsit.

The King of Prussia, as he passed our quarters, stopped to converse with us. The letter-box of the regiment, which, in the field, is placed beside the colours, attracted his notice

"For what purpose is that box?" asked Frederick William.

"Sire, to receive the letters which each of us writes to France."

"When you are in the field, is your post so organized as to convey the letters of all the soldiers?"

"Yes, sire; it goes out every day, it comes in every day; and we receive the Paris papers in a fortnight."

"It is admirable! For the rest, gentlemen, it is impossible to construct finer camps than yours; but, you must admit that you make deplorable villages."

The Queen of Prussia came to Tilsit. Napoleon was very attentive to her. All those assembled sovereigns, going out together every day, eating at the same table, appearing, in short, like old friends, though, but a few days before, they had been vituperating one another in their official gazettes, weapons more dangerous for kings than cannon, furnished a singular spectacle to an observer. For the rest, this friendship of recent date seemed to be cordial between Alexander and Napoleon; and, if one may ever trust to appearances in politics, it is probable that at Tilsit the parties were sincere. The Queen of Prussia was very handsome, for I saw her; she was said to be very amiable; on that point I can say nothing; but it is certain that she obtained many concessions from Napoleon. This beautiful princess, dining one day with the three sòvereigns, filled her glass with champagne, and said, with that grace which she possessed in a supreme degree: " To the health of Napoleon the great! he conquered our dominions, he restores them to us!" The emperor rose, courteously returned the compliment, and replied to the queen: "Do not drink the whole, madam!"

The sojourn in camp is ruinous to the officers; in general they prefer the bivouac, the position of which is changing every day. In the latter case, they live as they can, without having occasion to incur expense; whereas, the listlessness of a camp life causes them to frequent the suttler's coffee-room, or even to visit the neighbouring town, and the arrears of pay are consumed long before they are received.

After the armistice which followed the battle of Znaim, the whole party encamped till the conclusion of peace. We were in the environs of Brunn and Austerlitz, on the old field of battle. Frequently, in digging, fragments of arms and human bones were turned up. Napoleon resolved to give a repetition of the battle of Austerlitz. One fine day in September, the army occupied the same positions and made the same manœuvres as had taken place four years before. Everything passed off extremely well; the regiments which represented Austrian or Russian corps suffered themselves to be vanquished, as had been previously agreed upon, and nobody was drowned in the famous lake of Sokolnitz, which was not frozen.

The most favourable spot for pitching a camp is always in the vicinity of some handsome mansion, which may serve for head-quarters: the staff once comfortably settled, everything goes on smoothly.

A regiment, encamped, ought to occupy the same space as when under arms. Each company has in general six sheds, in three rows. Opposite to the centre of these sheds, and in rear of them, are placed the kitchens, built of turf, with walls and epaulements so constructed as to prevent sparks of fire from flying upon the straw-roofs. Farther on are the captain's shed and that of the lieutenants; still farther, that of the *chef de bataillon;* and, beyond them all, that of the colonel, placed opposite to the centre of the regiment.

The colonel's barrack is there, but it is usually unoccupied; those gentlemen prefer lodging at the next village, that is to say, when the enemy is at a distance, or when peace is concluded; for, during active hostilities, they are with the men night and day.

In camp, the officers dine either at the suttler's, where an ordinary is kept, or at their own quarters, where several mess together. In each company there is always a soldier who can cook tolerably well; and then, upon occasion, all lend a hand, and the result is frequently a delicious repast.

In the field, the officers are entitled to distributions of provisions. They receive their rations of bread, meat, salt, rice, &c. When eight or ten mess together, and know how to manage, they may live extremely well, provided they obtain a few supplementary articles from the next town.

In camp, the day is spent in visits to the soldiers' messes, inspections, parades, exercises, manœuvres—an extremely agreeable life, certainly, for those who are fond of it. In leisure moments, when the officer has books, he can read; when he has none, he walks about, and then at night he plays, and drinks mulled wine, amidst the smoke of pipes. This takes place either in the suttler's tent, or in the barrack of each officer in turn.

In some regiments, the colonels forbade play; in many others they tolerated it, because, being gamesters themselves, they wanted somebody to play with.

The usual games were *bouillote, imperiale,* and *vingt-un;* and at these amusements many a man lost his pay for a year. An officer of dragoons, whom I knew well, never stirred from the tent of the suttler who was most in vogue. Always ready to challenge the first comer to any game whatever he carried about him a well filled purse, the contents of which he displayed to excite the cupidity of the spectators.

One evening all his louis changed master: though he played extremely well, he lost everything. Fortune is fickle; she is not a female for nothing. The officer, in a thundering voice, called the suttler, and desired her to bring him a knife.

" What do you want it for ?"

" That is nothing to you—a knife, quick !"

A knife was accordingly brought, and he cut a great slash on his left side. We ran to him, affrighted, to disarm him.

" What ails you ?" cried he, laughing. " Sit down, and let me have my revenge."

" But you are wounded !"

" Wounded ! not such an idiot, faith ! I cut my waistcoat, that is all. I was obliged to release these unhappy prisoners."

In fact, the louis, the napoleons, the frederics d'or, poured in hundreds from the slit which had so terrified us. He played again, and soon won back all that he had lost.

This officer declared that, of all earthly pleasures, play was the greatest. " Men dare not avow that they are fond of play," said he; "people have but little esteem for a man who is addicted to it. He loses the confidence of others; every one cries: 'He is a gambler.' On the other hand, merchants, owners of privateers, are held in estimation; yet they run great risks, they gamble in reality, and sometimes with the money of others, which is not right. The Emperor Napoleon is the greatest gambler that I know; more than four times he has staked his all, and he is ever ready to begin afresh. As for me, nothing gives me such a relish for life as the chance of play. If I were not to play, I should be dead in a fortnight. Every morning and every night I say my prayers, like a good Christian, and always conclude with these words: 'O, God, let me be always playing and always winning!'"

A philosophical officer observed to him, one day, that play would be a very bad thing, were it only for the loss of time that it occasions. "You are right," replied our dragoon, with admirable coolness, "one does lose a great deal of time in shuffling the cards."

If the officers play for money, the men play for fillips. Nothing is more diverting than to see an old soldier receive them on his nose. Sometimes they are administered by a youngster, but even then the greybeard takes them without complaining, though not without making a very droll grimace. And then, to vary their amusement, they play at what they call *la drogue,* the loser having to carry, for a certain time, at the end of his nose, a pair of wooden pincers, which compress the nostrils. You may frequently have noticed little scenes of this kind in passing a *corps de garde,* or in turning over Charles's designs.

CHAPTER VIII.

THE GARRISON.

The military exercise is a very diverting thing. After a man has performed it for twenty, thirty years, he must still continue to go through it every day while he is in the service. When he does not know it, he must learn it; that is a matter of course: when he does know it, he must instruct others; this is just: and when the whole regiment manœuvres cleverly, it must still be performed to show its cleverness. Thus the exercise must be incessantly performed. An officer is continually going to or coming from it.

The exercise annoyed me a good deal, but I could conceive why, when one knew it, there was still a necessity for performing it, either to teach others, or not to forget it one's self. But a thing that I never could digest, a thing that was as disagreeable to me on the first day as on the last, was the parade. How, in fact, is it possible to conceive that rational creatures should be obliged to assemble daily at noon in a public place, to see about fifty heroes at thirty-five centimes per day file off for the guard-house, which they are to occupy for the next twenty-four hours! And yet I have known officers to whom the parade was as necessary as food, and who would have felt uncomfortable all day without their ordinary or their grand parade. When over, the general turns about, and says to you:—"Gentlemen, nothing new." Each then goes his way till the hour for exercise.

Next to the exercise and the parade, the *theory* must be classed among the agreeables of the profession. That theory consists in an examination, held daily by an officer, who asks you questions relative to some part of the "Instructions for the Soldier, the Platoon, or the Battalion." You see old officers with grey moustaches, who have been thirty years in the service, saying their lessons like young collegians. The college and the regiment are, indeed, very much alike; there are the same fears, the same passions, the same rivalries, only on a larger scale in the latter. By dint of reading and repeating this theory, you at last learned it, and knew it as thoroughly as the inventor. In this case, possessing certain patronage, you might be exempted from the periodical examinations: but, from the parade, from the exercise, nothing can release you; there each must pay in person. These occupy four or five hours a day; so you may easily calculate how many well-spent hours during thirty years' service.

In garrison, the coffee-houses, billiards, offer a great resource: there the officer spends almost all the time that is not devoted to the military service. I say almost, because the ladies claim a part, and that part is, certainly, the best employed. But, among the officers of a regiment, you find many who disdain that kind of enjoyment. To make love appears to them too great a trouble; they prefer buying it ready-made: every man to his taste in this world.

The officers meet at the coffee-house before they go to parade, to the exercise, or in returning from them. There are retailed the news of the army, of the regiment, and the gossip of the barracks. They play, they drink, they smoke: an officer is always ready to engage in a game at billiards, to smoke a cigar, to take a *petit verre*. The *petit verre* is a thing which young men who have recently put on the uniform would not dare to refuse; they would be afraid, lest they should pass for milksops. Dram-drinking is an essentially military practice. These habits are prejudicial to health, everybody knows, but everybody likes to do what is done by others. For a long time I drank regularly my three or four drams a day.

These pleasures, if pleasures they be, are the consequence of inoccupation, and they are very costly. It is not uncommon to see officers who spend their month's pay beforehand upon them. I have often been in this predicament: what I received has not been sufficient to discharge my running account at the coffee-house of the garrison.

When we arrived in a garrison, our first business was to seek a female with whom we could pass our time. As soon as we had found one, our minds were at rest. "Such a one has got his daily bread," was the expression used in the regiment when an officer had suited himself in this way. Sometimes these connexions terminated in a deplorable manner. Quarrels ensued with relatives, with rivals: swords were drawn—a disagreeable thing—because the result, be it what it will, always leaves behind it painful recollections in the mind of an honest man.

One of my friends, when at Ulm, had an adventure, the remembrance of which, even to this day, fills his heart with grief. He was on the most intimate terms with a young lady, whose parents were people of the first consequence in that city. They met at his quarters. After everybody had retired to rest, the lady stole out by the garden-gate, hastened to her lover, staid with him till daybreak, and then returned to her own home. This intrigue had been carried on for some time, and not a creature had the slightest suspicion of it. One morning my friend awoke just when it began to be light. "Make haste, my dear friend," said he; "it is time to go." No answer was returned: he touched her, she felt cold; he examined her, she was dead!

He doted on his mistress; conceive, then, his horror! What was to be done? the situation was dreadful. He rose, dressed, and ran to one of his friends, who was quartered on the parents of the poor girl, to ask his advice. His friend roused the father. "Sir," said he, "I have painful news to tell you—the most painful that you could receive: I have not time to prepare your heart for the stroke that impends over it. You suppose your daughter to be asleep in her own bed. Unhappy father! I am obliged to undeceive you. She is in the bed of one of my friends; she sleeps, but will never wake more; in short, she died last night in an attack of apoplexy."

" Gracious God! what is it you say?"

" Unfortunately the truth, the literal truth; but we have no time for lamentation. We must save the honour of your family; the scandal of such an event must, if possible, be avoided. My friend, whose anguish is equal to yours, knows no more what to do than you; I alone am capable of acting; leave the affair to me. I will send for the corpse of your daughter; she shall be well wrapped up; a soldier, for whose discretion I will be answerable, shall bring her to me as a bale of military effects, and we will carry her to her own bed, before a creature in your house knows anything of the matter. You must stay up to open the doors for us: should any of your people come down stairs, send them off immediately on some errand or other. Let us lose no time; I will go, and I answer for the result."

Everything was done as he had planned. The father appeared to know nothing of his daughter's death, till her maid entered her chamber. The whole town believed that she had expired in her own bed, and even her mother never conceived the slightest suspicion of the truth, the knowledge of which would have greatly increased the poignancy of her grief.

When we were to remain long in garrison, we had two grand resources for passing a merry life. If there was a lodge of freemasons, we went thither *en masse*, or we formed one of ourselves. Everybody knows that, while labouring at the great work, the brethren are fond of fun and feasting. In many of the regiments the officers formed a lodge, of which the colonel was master.

One of our comrades made game on all occasions of freemasons and freemasonry. "Our proofs," he said, "were only fit to frighten children," and when he was urged to apply for admission, he answered with a grin:—"I am too old a boy to play at chapel."

However, as our parties of pleasure were confined to the initiated, he was not only excluded from them, but heard on the morrow a highly exaggerated account of the doings of the preceding day. This piqued his curiosity; he grew tired of amusing himself all alone, and solicited admission into the jovial band. He was then told to prepare himself for the severest trial that had been imposed in the memory of man. He defied us to frighten him for a moment.

The important day at length arrived; all our batteries were prepared. Our candidate had just been consigned to the closet of reflection, when the house in which the lodge was held caught fire. To terminate the day in a manner essentially masonic, a grand dinner was preparing. The kitchen presented a magnificent sight; the fires were blazing, and the scullions running in all directions to execute the orders of the head-cook. A chimney, which for a long time had not been visited by a sweep, caught fire. It communicated to the upper floors; the *generale* was beat, the garrison got under arms, the engines arrived, and poured forth torrents of water to extinguish the flames.

Meanwhile, our candidate was still in the closet of reflection. We had forgotten him at first, and afterwards concluded that the fire would drive him out. He, however, kept his post without flinching. Luckily, the flames did not spread his way, or he would certainly have been burned alive. If he was not roasted, at any rate he was completely drenched, for an engine-pipe, playing right at his head, gave him as fine a ducking as ever cooled the brain of a maniac. "'Tis of no use," he cried; "you will not frighten me with your straw fires; I have seen far different at Hohenlinden, at Austerlitz, at Jena," and so he went on, repeating, amidst the smoke, the catalogue of the battles in which he had been.

The firemen were obliged to turn him out by force, otherwise, I dare say, he would have been there still. "You would never have frightened me with your silly proofs," said he, as he went down stairs, "but you might have stifled me. Who knows but I may catch a fine cold by it! This is beyond a joke, gentlemen; I am as wet as if I had been in the river." It was a long time before they could make him comprehend the truth, and convince him that the fire was not a mere frolic; for we were not accustomed to roast our adepts, in order to make them keep a secret.

Next to freemasonry came the drama, which furnishes an excellent pastime when one is young. At Magdeburg, the playhouse was occupied by a company of bad German actors; they refused to give it up to us, so we metamorphosed a magazine of forage into a theatre. At that time the garrison was twenty-five thousand strong. Each officer contributed a month's pay to defray the expense of lighting, dresses, and decorations. Our theatre was soon organized, provided with machinery and with every requisite. Be it understood, that no money was paid at the door, and that we were always applauded. Tickets were distributed in the city; we had always a full house, that is to say, all the agreeables of the profession without its inconveniences. Add to this that the wives of the officers, the commissaries, and the clerks of the victualling department, who performed along with us, were very amiable women.

The officer-actors never did any duty. As the time which they spent in the theatre was devoted to the pleasures of their comrades, the latter mounted guard for them, commanded the exercise, and all were satisfied. We performed pieces of every class—tragedy, comedy, opera, and farce. The orchestra, selected from the bands of all the regiments, was perfect. Many pieces were as well acted on our stage at Magdeburg, as in the first theatres of France. We received all the new pieces from Paris; they were immediately studied, and were brought out as soon as at Lyons, Rouen, or Bordeaux. The poor German actors could not stand the competition with comedians who performed gratuitously, and went to seek their fortune elsewhere.

One day, the curtain was raised on the individual account of one of our young actors. He bowed thrice to his audience. "Gentlemen," said he, "I have just had a pair of white cassimere breeches, which cost me forty francs, utterly spoiled; a whole lampful of oil has been spilt over them. You may easily conceive how much this must have ruffled my temper. The idea will, no doubt, annoy me while I am performing my part; I have, therefore, to solicit your indulgence, if I should not play so well as usual."

What bickerings, what rivalries, what gossip, what slander, behind our scenes? If we had been so fortunate as to have a newspaper or two at Magdeburg, their columns would have overflowed with piquant adventures. From all that I have seen in our dramatic company, I might even say from all I have myself done, I have deduced one aphorism, which I advise all husbands to note down in their tablets. It is this: "When a wife plays in private theatricals, the honour of the husband (since honour there is) loses in direct proportion to the pleasure that she takes in them."

The wife of a general, whom I shall not name, had formerly been an actress at the Théâtre Montausier in Paris. Having become a baroness of the empire, she took good care to say nothing about her former profession. All these ladies, who ridiculed the *marquises* of the Faubourg St. Germain, were particularly anxious to imitate them. The baroness, a clever comedian, had copied them pretty closely, and given herself great airs, which were highly displeasing to the lady-captains.

Spiteful people meanwhile whispered to one another the reason why the general had married her; they talked of her conduct before marriage, ay, and afterwards, too: but the lady was handsome and amiable; we listened not to their evil tongues, the women alone triumphed over these indiscretions. She took it into her head to act in farce; she chose her parts (a general's lady had a right to choose), and she performed them admirably. Old habits got the better of her; she assumed the sceptre at repetitions: the love of rule took possession of her feminine heart; the barony was forgotten; and, in the hope of reigning as sovereign on our boards, she confessed that, having acted in Paris, nobody was better qualified than herself to direct our operations. Thenceforward all that the general lost on the side of vanity, she won on that of power, and to women that compensation is always sufficient.

The other ladies consoled themselves by a deluge of epigrams, of which the general's lady, covered with the honours of the management, took no notice. With her, as the arbitress of our pleasures, we all made interest for a part, and some even solicited the grant of two. Creating reputations, her words were decrees, fixed as those of Fate.

Her success in farce induced the baroness to aspire to a higher sphere. She resolved to wear the buskin, personated Phedra, Rodane, &c.: but a wide gulf separates the flimflams of Desaugiers from the pompous speeches of Racine. Nevertheless, those who had never seen tragedy performed in Paris admired the baroness in Phedra.

The Magdeburgers, who were not fond of us, were gratified when we invited them to our representations; I dare say that their city never was so brilliant as at that time. We also gave balls, and, of all possible balls, those in garrison are certainly the finest. The variety of the military costumes produces a charming effect, especially when there are regiments of all arms. Look at a ball in Paris: the ladies vie with one another in the elegance of their dresses; they display the most beautiful and the most diversified colours; there is a profusion of gold, silk, blond, gauze: the gentlemen, on the contrary, habited in black, and nothing but black, all look as if they had just come from a funeral. We ought, at length, to adopt a different costume for such different circumstances; but, so long as we take the English for our models, we shall not dare to step out of the beaten track.

The French have a singular mania; they laugh at the English by the day together; when they bring an Englishman upon their stage, he is almost always a ludicrous character. John Bull is the burlesque hero of innumerable caricatures; and yet, the moment a fashion is imported from England, our exquisites and our fine ladies never fail to catch it up. What am I talking of! we imitate them at dinner, ay, even at dinner! To what purpose have we raised the gastronomic art to the summit of its glory, to what purpose have we set ourselves up for a model to the whole eating world, if, returning to the point from which we started, we copy the repasts of Ajax and Diomed, by devouring an ox roasted whole! Return, my dear countrymen, I beseech you, to our delicate little French dishes; relinquish those substantial viands, worthy of the Greek heroes of the olden time, and of the carmen of the present day!

The fashion! the fashion! you will cry, and you are perfectly right. The chief point is not to amuse yourselves, but to make people believe that you are amused. You might have a comfortable party by assembling sixty persons in your saloon: you must invite four hundred to have a rout Every one of them will be nearly stifled: what signifies that, so the fashion is followed? We have need of orthodox pleasures; our pleasures must be deemed pleasures by the fashionable world; were we to amuse ourselves *in petto*, we should not be amused at all. A lover of good cheer said one day to the most celebrated gastronome of our age: " I have made an excellent dinner."—" That is not so certain," replied the latter, with admirable coolness; " tell me what you have eaten, and I will tell you whether you have had a good dinner."

But to return to our garrison-balls; they were just like those at Paris—plenty of walking, but very little dancing. From system, we collected as much company as possible, so that the inamoratoes—and they abounded in our regiments—were nearer to their fair ones, and the mammas, separated from their daughters by a wall of uniforms, could not see anything. Billets-doux were interchanged; squeezes of the hand, amorous glances, delicious half-words, usurped the place of the dance, and everybody declared that the ball was charming.

With the women it is precisely the same: the ball is but a pretext, an occasion, for seeing the happy man, whom there is no hope of meeting elsewhere. And besides, in a drawing-room a tender interview would be too much noticed; whereas dancing, music, the bustle, the crowd, effect a useful diversion. At the ball, women appear with all their advantages, to say nothing of those of dress; they can walk, leap, come, go, instead of being chained down to their seats, with bodies upright as heads of asparagus, a tiresome and not over and above graceful position. Look a lady in the face; the next moment, you will see her turn her head, that you may have an opportunity of admiring her profile.

Observe that knot of young ladies in a saloon; they are embroidering, reading, chatting, and as seriously as possible. A young gentleman comes in: all at once they begin to whisper; they seem to be saying the funniest things to one another, for they are giggling heartily. And yet they have said nothing; but their countenances have become animated, and this enhances the brightness of a fine pair of eyes. If, when the visitor entered, the shoulders of these young ladies were covered with a shawl, be sure that in five minutes, without the least fear of catching cold, they will have got rid of everything that could prevent him from admiring the elegance of their shapes. A hundred times have I made this observation, and as often has the shawl slipped down behind the chair.

CHAPTER IX.

BARRACKS.

THE conscript, whom the lot snatches from the paternal home, leaves it weeping; once at barracks, all is forgotten. Fearing the jeers of his comrades, he has soon dried his tears: a trait of ridicule is more terrible to us Frenchmen than the cut of a sword. When the novice is measured, numbered, clothed from head to foot, you would take him at a distance for one of the heroes of Austerlitz. But, on a closer view, you think differently: his manner is stiff; he knows not what to do with his arms; his legs are in his way; and the bumpkin, when he walks, always has a stick in his hand to keep him in countenance.

Meanwhile the instructor arrives: this is some moustached corporal, a famous talker, who, in the intervals of rest between the hours of exercise, never fails to relate to the youngster all the exploits that formerly shed a lustre upon his name. The conscript listens, open-mouthed, and cannot conceive how it happens that the corporal is not yet a colonel. The neglect of so illustrious a soldier serves to discourage himself.

The conscript, on quitting the plough, conceives that at the barracks he shall encounter all the miseries of human life. "You will be half-starved," he has been told a hundred times. He is quite astonished to have wholesome beef, flanked with a sufficient quantity of potatoes, and his everyday fare is better than that which he had at his father's on Sundays. His bread is good, and whiter than that eaten in three-fourths of the villages of France.

The soldier is a man possessing his income of twelve hundred francs, net and clear, without bankruptcy, without repairs, without imposts, without protested bills. I have calculated the value of his lodging, his food, his clothes, his fuel, his moveables, which he is constantly using, but which he never renews; and from all my figures I have concluded that many *rentiers* do not live so well, and, above all, so free from care as the soldier. If he is ill, his physicians in ordinary, his surgeons in embroidered clothes, take pleasure in attending him for nothing; the apothecary supplies him gratis with ipecacuanha and bark; leeches, brought at a great expense from Hungary, are in readiness to be placed on all the parts directed by the medical officers.

Our sick-nurses must have, over and above their wages, well filled sugar-boxes, which they are incessantly emptying, bottles of all sorts, broths without end, and still they grumble from morning till night. Nothing is given to the keeper of the infirmary; on the contrary, if the soldier knows how to manage, when he becomes convalescent, he will have the best soup, the pullet's wing, and the half-bottle of choice wine.

And then, in addition to all these advantages, consider the beatitudes of the daily *sou* for pocket-money; the sou which is incessantly coming, incessantly going; a fertile, an inexhaustible mine, supplying all sorts of pleasures, from the glass of brandy to the pipe of tobacco. A new wandering Jew, the soldier continually finds the daily sou at the bottom of his pocket. Let the sou wait patiently for its brethren, which never fail at the appointed rendezvous, and next Sunday, after the parade, a juicy pork-chop, and delicious wine, at six sous per pint, will furnish, beyond the barrier, a regale that will be the more relished the less frequently it occurs. The soldier always lodges in the best building in the town. Go to St. Denis, ask for the finest edifice—it is the barracks.

At Vincennes, the soldiers inhabit the apartments of our kings; at Avignon, they are installed in the palace of the popes. Well clothed, well warmed, well lodged, well fed—what lacks the soldier? Oh! but a mere trifle, as the dog in the fable said to his companion—liberty. That collar which is riveted about the neck of the soldier is not broken till he is released from the service, either by a discharge or by a cannon-ball. All the time that the soldier passes with the regiment is divided into a hundred different portions, scarcely one of which belongs exclusively to himself. If he sleeps, the drum awakes him; if he wakes, the drum obliges him to sleep. The drum makes him march; it stops him, leads him to exercise, to battle, to mass, to the promenade. "I am hungry."—"You must be mistaken, my friend; the drum has not yet made that rolling which ought alone to shake the fibres of your stomach. The soup cannot be ready till the drum has said so."—"If I had but a crust of bread!" "Dolt! the drum has not beat the *breloque*."*

In the morning, the soldier, broom in hand, sweeps the barracks within and without; and again the drum calls him to his duty. One day, in Laborie's week, when, of course, he had to superintend the sweepers, he was very angry with a corporal, because a heap of dirt, for the removal of which he had given positive orders the day before, had not been taken away.

"But, lieutenant, we know not where to put it."

"Throw it outside."

"The mayor has already complained, and the colonel forbidden that to be done."

---

* The *breloque* is a beat of the drum, to call together the fatigue-parties, charged to receive the allowances of provisions.

"Well, then, dig a hole and bury it."

"And what shall we do with the mould that comes out of it?"

"Are you stupid, corporal? you must make it large enough to hold both."

When the sweeping is finished, the manual exercise succeeds; and then the arms and accoutrements must be cleaned, the cartouch-box polished, the clothes brushed, the shoes blacked, the buttons brightened. Make haste, it is the hour for the parade. It is there you must shine. Come along, my hero, distinguish yourself; the least spot on your frock would draw a prohibition to go out upon the corporal of the week and the sergeant of the week, arrest upon the lieutenant of the week, and you would long feel the effects of the punishment which they had undergone for your sake. These gentlemen are civilly responsible for the appearance of their soldiers. "If they are not smart," says the colonel, "it is you that I shall call to account."

All these orders of the drum, of the corporal, and of the officers, must always be obeyed instantly, without remark, without reply. When the clock-maker has made a clock, it goes without asking why. Soldier, you must be like the clock; march, turn, halt, and above all not a word!

"But, captain . . . ."

"To the *salle de police* for two days."

"If you would but listen to me . . . ."

"For four days."

"And yet . . . ."

"For a week."

"It is an injustice!"

"To prison for a fortnight. If you say another word, beware of the black hole and a court-martial."

Such is the summary justice of the regiment; men get used to it as to everything else. As soon as a young soldier has had a taste of the *salle de police*, it makes a difference, and he profits for the future by the lesson. I except those depraved, incorrigible fellows, those gaol-birds, who are doomed at last to drag the cannon-ball, or to be shot.

Nothing short of this severity has been necessarily required, in order that one individual might be master of one hundred thousand armed men. Passive obedience from grade to grade is the condition, *sine qua non* of the existence of an army. The most absurd, the most stupid, order must be obeyed without a word. What could be done, if each were to arrogate to himself the right to give advice? We all imagine that we possess abundance of good sense; in our own minds we often set down our neighbour for an idiot, and he does the same on his part by us. A military chief, who should consult his officers, who should merely listen to their remonstrances, would never be sure of the execution of an order. This would modify it; that would fancy he was saving the army by doing the contrary.

In 1813, we were in the environs of Berlin: we were effecting our retreat, which was not very agreeable, for, in order to see the Russians, we were obliged to make a half-turn. One evening, the general received a letter to this effect. I must first mention that we were quartered in a village, with two battalions and four pieces of cannon, and that we were face to face with the enemy.

"My dear general, send immediately one of your battalions to the village of ―――――. The officer who commands it must guard himself militarily, and keep up all night patroles which are to communicate with ours. Give him two of your pieces of cannon."

Assuredly this order was positive enough; never was there anything less ambiguous. Our general gave orders for the departure of the battalion; he read the letter again and again, mused over it, and then exclaimed: "He does not say what I am to do with the other two pieces of cannon."

"You must keep them, of course."

"His letter does not say so."

"Neither does it say what you are to do with the other battalion. You must keep the battalion and the cannon too."

The general was perhaps vexed to see that I was clearly right. He takes me for a fool? said he to himself. Soho, my fine fellow, who fancy yourself a deal cleverer than I am. I'll make you smart for it! "Mount your horse, sir; go to the general of division, and ask him the meaning of his letter."

"But it seems to me that . . ."

"Let the order I give you be instantly obeyed."

"Be assured, general, that it is useless; that I always do my duty with zeal, but that at this moment . . ."

"Be gone, sir, I command you."

"I was obliged to start, to run all night through fields, along horrible roads with which I was not acquainted: the rain poured in torrents, and I assure you that the ride was none of the most agreeable. I had to pass through all the French sentries: twice or thrice I got in the dark to the enemy's advanced posts, and musket-shots drove me back into my road. The French, hearing me coming from the wrong direction, fired upon me too, long before they cried *Qui vive!* which they are too much in the habit of doing. If I escaped with my life that night, it was entirely owing to the terrible weather, which I heartily cursed at the moment of my departure. At length, I arrived at the quarters of the general of division, at Köpnick.

"Where is the general? waken the general! I must speak to the general."

"What is the matter, then? Are we attacked?" asked the officers of the staff.

"Waken the general. I am ordered to speak to none but himself."

The brave ―――― was enjoying the sweets of his first

sleep. I entered his chamber, with my sabre trailing along the floor.

"Ah! you there! Is there fighting in your quarter? Do you come for reinforcement?"

"I am come to inquire the meaning of your order."

"What order?"

"Our general wishes to know what he is to do with the two pieces of cannon that he has left."

"Are you making game of me?"

"Most certainly I should not take such a liberty. I hope, general, that you think me incapable of doing so."

"Then you must be silly."

"Permit me, general, to remark that I am not acting on my own account; that I am merely the bearer of a message from another. This other asks, by my voice, what he is to do with the two pieces of cannon."

"Are we acting a play? or is it a wager that you are striving to win?"

"Believe me, general, if I were acting the play, I would not take the liberty to make you an interlocutor without your permission; and, if I had laid a wager, I should not have dared to waken you in the middle of the night to decide the losing or the winning of it. Once more I repeat my question: What are we to do with the two pieces of cannon that we have left?"

"Go to the devil with them!"

"So much for myself; but the general?"

"Well, both of you, together or separately; I care not how: let me alone; I want to sleep."

My embassy finished, I mounted my horse again, and got back by eight in the morning, at the very moment when the battalion and the two fatal pieces of cannon were on the point of starting. The general was at the head of his troops. I arrived, bowed to him, and waited to be questioned.

"Have you seen the general of division?"

"Yes."

"What says he?"

"Something which I dare not repeat."

"I insist on knowing!"

"Military subordination forbids me to reply."

"Military subordination, sir, orders you to obey me! What said the general to you?"

"He desired me to tell you to go to the devil."

"Sir!"

"General, twenty witnesses heard him, and here are hundreds more to declare that you have ordered me to speak."

This passive subordination, this necessary obedience, is sometimes most injurious; but things would be much worse if it did not exist. In the campaign of 1814, when so many excellent veteran troops had been left by the emperor in the fortresses on the Elbe and the Oder, as far as Dantzick, if a general had dared to quit the place committed to his keeping, and then marched to the other towns, collecting the garrisons as he proceeded, what an immense diversion might he not have operated!

The thing was not so difficult as one might imagine. The idea occured to all the generals, but all of them shrunk from the moral responsibility which they would have incurred. Marshal Davoust might have left Hamburg with twenty thousand men, and marched to Magdeburg, where General Lemarrois would have joined him with twelve thousand, proceeding together to the garrisons on the Elbe and the Oder, those two officers would have picked up, every two or three days, fresh reinforcements. No doubt they would have met with obstacles by the way, but they would have defied them. They were afraid of only one thing—not obeying punctually the orders which they had received.

The greatest efforts of the allies were directed against Napoleon; all their best troops were in France. The soldiers of the new levies blockaded the fortresses; the landwehr and the landsturm were there doing their first duty; they must have opened their ranks, whether they would or not, to allow our troops a free passage. Conceive the effect which these tidings would have produced in France after the battle of Brienne, or that of Montmirail. Figure to yourself the French army entering Berlin on the same day that the allies entered Paris.

In a discussion between a superior and an inferior, the latter can never be more in the wrong than when he is right.

In the army I have known very clever officers, who practised absolute self-denial, gave way to all sorts of caprices, made themselves the counsellors of high personages, and never let it be supposed that they had suggested good advice. This is the quintessence of the courtier's art: everybody could not attain that point.

Many generals wished to play the part of princes. The uniform of the aides-de-camp was a blue frock, with sky-blue collar and trimmings. Almost all the servants of the generals were dressed in the same manner, only without the epaulette. Thus there was a regular establishment of servants of all grades: captain, lieutenant, valet, groom, &c. These aristocratic manners had succeeded the republican austerity without any gradual transition. I have known aides-de-camp who submitted with admirable grace to all these hierarchical servitudes; they had precedence of the valet, and that was enough for them. On the other hand, I have known generals who carried reserve to the utmost scrupulousness. Never would they have required of officers under their command a service that was not within the sphere of their military duties.

I arrived one day, with General P——, at an uninhabited house; a heavy rain was falling, and we were wet through. We lighted a fire and warmed ourselves.

"Sit down there," said the general to me.

"What for?"

"I will pull your boots off."

"You are joking."

"Not at all; give me hold of your foot."

"Indeed, general, I could not allow you."

"Your boots are soaked—your feet are wet; you will catch cold."

"But I will pull them off myself."

"I insist on pulling them off for you."

Whether I would or not, the general pulled off my boots. My astonishment was extreme. When he had finished: "One good turn," said he, "deserves another; now pull off my boots."

"With pleasure."

"In order to acquire the right to ask this service of you, how could I do otherwise?"

Barracks ought to be placed in an elevated situation, that they may not be damp, and that the air may circulate around such a mass of men collected together. There are very fine barracks in Paris, at Courbevoie, at St. Denis, and at Rueil. Some of them have been built expressly for the purpose; others are old convents, where the virgin spouses of the Lord sang the praises of God. If walls have ears, they must find some difference between these songs and those now sung there. The barracks at Avignon, some of the finest in France, were formerly inhabited by the popes. Part of their palace has been transformed into lodgings for soldiers. Never did masons pile stones upon stones with less taste. This palace, to which all the sovereign pontiffs of Avignon contributed without ever finishing it, exhibits a truly singular aspect: towers of prodigous height, immense halls, several churches, enclosed within walls eighteen feet thick—all erected without definite aim or plan. At the time of the wars in Italy, between the Guelphs and the Ghibellines, the popes took refuge in Avignon, and for the seventy years that they resided there, each persisted in adding fresh stones to the stones piled up by his predecessors.

It must not be imagined that the soldier in barracks leads an idle life. His duties employ him in such a manner, that his only recreation consists in change of labour. Fatigue parties for the general cleansing of the building and the courts, the cleaning of arms and of clothes, the exercise, mounting guard, all succeed one another periodically, so that the soldier is never long without something to do.

In barracks the soldier reads a good deal in leisure moments. You are sure to see a circulating library near the spot where a regiment is quartered. Go in, you will easily discover the favourite books by the thick coat of dirt on the back. I was one day with the mistress of the shop, when a young conscript entered, switch in hand.

" Have you Robert, the Chief of Banditti ?"

" No, sir, it is out."

" Have you Rinaldo Rinaldini ?"

" No, sir; your comrades are reading it."

" Have you . . . . but I forget the titles; look me out some other book about robbers."

Five or six, sometimes the whole squad, join to pay for such a set of books, and one of them reads aloud to the rest. It is amusing to see all those worthy troopers, listening, open-mouthed, to the wonderful stories of Cartouche, Mandrin, or La Ramée. Not that the soldiers feel a sort of sympathy for robbers; but the adventurous life of the latter bears some resemblance to the episodes and the dangers of the career of glory. They would rather read the history of robbers than of heroes; the latter they know by heart; they learned the story of all our campaigns, of all our battles, without loosing their purse-strings. In every mess you find a veteran who has seen everything, and who never misses an opportunity of relating his exploits. In each company there is a man of this kind, whose moral influence over his comrades is very powerful. It is he who criticizes all the operations of the captain. "In my old regiment," he says, "they never did this or that." His old regiment is his stalking-horse; it is the pattern which all ought to follow. When he is removed to another corps, that which he has just left will become the model in its turn, for he cannot set up two, and the last will always be the best.

In the barracks there is always a pavilion for lodging a certain number of officers: so large a flock must have some shepherds. In barracks you find dealers in wine, brandy, tobacco, sometimes billiard-tables, and restaurateurs. The suttler, after carrying the barrel, slung across her shoulder, along the high roads, rests herself in a corner of the ground-floor, pompously called the restaurant. Farther on is the coffee-house; you must not look there for the luxury of gilding, mirrors, and lustres of crystal. What signifies that! it offers to the sub-lieutenants a great advantage, which makes sufficient compensation; they get credit there till the end of the month, and, for some pockets, that is a great accommodation; at least, I have often found it so.

I have known suttlers, who, from one humble pot, have so increased their means as to have forty regular customers, whom they supplied with an excellent dinner. They began with dining four, then five, then ten, and their reputation spreading in the direct ratio of the excellence of their viands, they had, by and by, to provide for all the officers of a regiment.

The dinner-hour is often a very agreeable one. It is at table that you hear the news of the regiment and of the army; there, too, you sometimes settle the destinies of Europe. Each grade has its separate table; otherwise, the familiarity which naturally insinuates itself among persons who eat together would be very prejudicial to subordination. Each of the guests have an account current in the great book of the restaurateur. He is debited with all the extras with which he indulges himself in the course of the month; the bill is frequently a very long one, the accessories exceeding the principal item.

And then, at the dessert, the company chat; and, when their military duties permit, continue a long time at table. These conversations have furnished me with some of the stories that I have related to you.

CHAPTER X.

REVIEWS.

A REVIEW is sometimes an entertaining sight to the spectators, seated or standing in the pit; but to the actors it is a very different sort of thing. The former may retire whenever they please; the latter must stay till the conclusion of the piece.

When the Emperor gave orders for a review at noon, the generals inspected the troops at eleven o'clock; the colonels had their regiments under arms at ten; *chefs de bataillon*, anxious previously to ascertain if all was right, began at nine; and so on in a decreasing proportion to the corporal, who had his squad afoot at five in the morning. This frequent getting under arms fatigues the soldier more than a day of battle. He knows that the battle is necessary, and goes to it cheerfully; as for the other, he sees that it might very well be dispensed with.

When the troops are on the ground, how many marches and counter-marches before each corps is definitively in its place! how many alignments taken and retaken before the Emperor arrives! At length the drums give the signal along the whole line: there he is! His small hat and green horse-chasseur's frock distinguish him amid the crowd of princes and generals, with embroidery on every seam.

People, now-a-days, talk of nothing but the love of the soldiers for Napoleon, of the acclamations, a thousand times repeated, that hailed him as he passed: it is perhaps wrong in me to contradict a thing affirmed by so many illustrious persons, but I must say, and I do say, that these acclamations were very rare. There was plenty of fighting at the grand army, but little shouting, though a great deal of grumbling.

We were in camp, under the walls of Tilsit; there was talk of peace, of an interview between the two emperors, and we walked to the banks of the Niemen, to see what was passing. When we arrived, the conference was over: the two boats, with the sovereigns on board, were proceeding towards the opposite sides of the river. The Emperor Alexander landed first; he was greeted by a general huzza from his troops. Napoleon appeared on our bank; Talleyrand gave him his arm to assist him to land. Not a cry was heard among the soldiers. Some of the officers, however, set the example. We all said to our neighbours, Napoleon ought not to be less cordially received by us than Alexander had been by the Russians; and we heard, here and there, some shouts of *Vive l'empereur !*

" His majesty is coming ;" said our colonel at the moment of a review. " I hope he will not be received as he was last time, and that the soldiers will cry *Vive l'empereur !* Look to it, gentlemen ; I shall hold you responsible if every man does not shout lustily." We returned to our companies, paraphrasing the colonel's harangue, and the following were among the murmurs that we heard in the ranks:

" Let him give me my discharge, and I'll shout as loud as they please."—" We have no bread; I can't shout upon an empty stomach."—" I was to return in six months, and here have I been twenty years in the army; let them send me home, and I'll shout."—" We are owed six months' pay; why don't we get it?"—" What a simpleton you must be!

why, I'll tell you: all those that get killed in the meantime are paid."

The emperor arrived: the colonel and some of the officers shouted as though they would split their throats; the rest were silent. I never saw the soldiers heartily cry *Vive l'empereur!* but in 1814 and 1815, when they were told to shout *Vive le roi!* I must say that then they shouted till they were hoarse: why?—the soldier is essentially a grumbler, either because he wishes from time to time to make himself some amends for his sheepish obedience, or because he is secretly envious of those who command him, as a servant is of his master, and a scholar of his instructor.

In 1815, a regiment was passing through a town in the South. The soldiers exhorted one another to shout *Vive l'empereur!* all together, and with all their might; the din was such as almost to split the drum of the ear, to break all the windows. After each round, they chuckled to themselves, saying: " Well done! that nettles the townspeople."

How often has it been asserted in print that the soldiers fought for the emperor! This is another of those current phrases, which many people have taken up and repeated without knowing why. The soldiers fought for themselves, to defend themselves; because, in France, a man never hesitates when he sees danger on one side and infamy on the other. They fought, because it was impossible to do otherwise; because it was necessary to fight; because, when they joined the army, they found the fashion of fighting established, and everything tending to keep up that good old practice. They fought under the old monarchy, with Turenne, Villars, and Marshal Saxe; under the republic, with Hoche, Moreau, Kleber, and many others; they will always fight when the country shall call upon them. Show them the Prussians, the Russians, or the Austrians, and whether they are commanded by Napoleon, Charles X., or Louis Philippe, you may be sure that French soldiers will do their duty.

I am aware, at the same time, that the presence of the emperor produced a powerful effect on the army. Every one had the most implicit confidence in him; every one knew, from experience, that his plans led to victory, and therefore, when he did arrive, our moral force was doubled. But this endless succession of actions and battles wearied many of the old soldiers, of the old officers, of the old generals: they scrupled not to say so; but not one failed, on this account, to do his duty when occasion presented itself.

During the empire, the soldiers wished for nothing so much as discharge, peace, return to France; as, at the present day, they are anxious for war, campaigns, bivouacs, and battles. They have returned to France; they have had peace and their discharge; what was the consequence? They regretted former times. Why? because the heart of man is constantly pushing forward to a future, which, when it has become the present, displeases, since it is no longer encompassed with clouds. How happy, said they, if we had peace! Now they cry: How happy, if we had war! Besides, I repeat it, the soldiers are grumblers; several of them, while enjoying the repose of civil life, were not sorry to appear to regret the tumult of the camp; each well knew that all these murmurs would not prevent things from pursuing their course, and he gave himself somewhat of the air of a hero in the neighbourhood. Meanwhile the lithographers line the Boulevards of Paris with portraits of old soldiers, with bushy moustaches, shedding tears on reading the word *congé* (discharge) on a placard. The innumerable cockneys of the capital deplored, in elegiac prose, the lot of our brave warriors, who were dismissed without pity, as if in France there were not at all times vacant places of private soldiers at the disposal of amateurs.

I was talking one day on this subject with a publisher of lithographic prints, and was beginning to prove what I am here advancing. "You preach to one who is already converted," said he at the first word : " I am well aware that all this is not true, but such things sell. In trade, ' such things sell' is an unanswerable argument. I lately published a lithographic print, representing ten of our grenadiers obliging two English battalions to lay down their arms. The names, the time, the place of action, are all of my invention. What signifies that! the thing was thought superb, and every day I sell hundreds of impressions. Go to a theatre, take notice of the couplets that are most applauded; they are those in which *Français* rhymes with *succés, gloire* with *victoire, guerriers* with *lauriers.* Observe the shopmen, exciting one another to applaud with a sort of frenzy; and yet, if you were to make inquiry, how many would you not find among these heroes of the pit, who had hid themselves in 1814 to avoid joining the army, and whom the Restoration relieved from the penalties incurred by refractory conscripts!"

The French have performed prodigies of valour, and, to use an expression of Napoleon's, they have made litter of glory; but it would not be amiss to let others say so; we ought not every day to give ourselves bloody noses by swinging the censer against them.

Napoleon was, without doubt, a consummate general; his campaigns in Italy border on the marvellous, for he had not then at his disposal the immense resources which he subsequently possessed. The battles of the empire made more noise, but they will never efface the glory of those which preceded them. Victory was the result in both cases, you may say. True, but merit is usually measured by the difficulty surmounted; and the glory of Bonaparte will never be eclipsed by that of Napoleon; for the means of the emperor were more vast than ever general had at his disposal. When a ruler drains a country like France of her last man and her last crown, when he renders an account to no one, it is not surprising that, with a well-organized head, he should accomplish great things; the contrary would be much more astonishing. Suppose Napoleon, with a representative government, such as we have at present; he would probably have been very quickly arrested in his victorious career. Now, eighty thousand conscripts are raised annually; but the statements for each department are published in the newspapers, and the total corresponds exactly with the number fixed by the law. During the empire, when one hundred thousand men were ostensibly demanded, three hundred thousand were actually raised; and among all the prefects this furnished a perpetual subject of emulation for attaining a seat in the council of state.

Now, what would Napoleon have done with a paltry conscription of one hundred thousand men? We will suppose that this number left France; eighty thousand at most would join the armies; half of these would, as usual, be in the hospitals in a week; forty thousand only could be brought into line, and forty thousand men would have been a mere trifle at a time when human life was so prodigally expended. They would scarcely have sufficed to defray the demands of a single battle: more than one might be mentioned which cost still dearer.

Suppose there had existed in Napoleon's time two free Chambers, and all the operations of the government checked, one by one, by a conscientious opposition. Suppose the ministers obliged to be perpetually thinking how to retain a majority in the Chambers, consequently devoting but half their time to the administration; suppose an innumerable multitude of newspapers acquainting the enemy with the indiscretions of the bureaux, the position of the troops, their marches, their *matériel*, the number of their cannon, of their baggage-waggons, of their men, of their drums; I doubt very much whether Napoleon would have been exalted by victory to the height that he was. But then the thirst of conquest would have been naturally allayed by the force of circumstances; and he, as well as we, in short, the whole world, would have been all the better for it. The liberty of the press is certainly an excellent thing; but more patriotism ought to prevail in the use that is daily made of it; we ought not to tell our neighbours what it is so important to them to know. The enemy formerly kept spies among us; he now obtains his intelligence at a much cheaper rate—he subscribes to our journals.

But I perceive that I am getting into politics, and I assure you that this was not my intention. Still, as I have begun to make suppositions, I will communicate to you an idea which frequently ambles through my head. At the time of the consulate, Louis XVIII. wrote to General Bonaparte to persuade him to give up the throne to him. "Choose," said he, "such places as you think fit for yourself and your friends." I frequently amuse myself with calculating what had been the consequence, had Napoleon complied with this proposal. Suppose Monsieur le Marquis de Bonaparte captain of the gardes-du-corps. Would the officers of the other companies have deigned to admit him?— they would not dine with Molière. When a gentleman had committed a fault, he would have been placed in Bonaparte's company.

What taunts would have been levelled at the vulgarity, the awkwardness, of the upstart, of the soldier of fortune! The lowest clown, nay, the lowest valet of the *grand seigneur*, would have deemed himself placed much higher in the court hierarchy: for be assured that the valet of a nobleman thinks himself far above an untitled person; the more cringing he is to an embroidered coat, the more insolent he behaves to a commoner dressed in black.

I picture my Bonaparte galloping by the side of the King's carriage from the Tuileries to Versailles, from St. Cloud to Rambouillet; I see him annoyed by the jeers of the right noble courtiers; I figure to myself the latter blasted by a flash of his eye, turning on their red heels, and saying: "What an ill-bred fellow!" Would he have had the red ribbon? I doubt it. I laugh when I think of the catastrophe that would necessarily have terminated the fifth act of this comedy. One fine day, our fresh-dubbed marquis would have marched up a few companies of his old Egyptians, and then—room there! every one take care of himself!—the whole system would have vanished like a dream. It is really a pity that we did not see this—we who have seen so many extraordinary things.

At every review the Emperor appointed to vacant places, and conferred crosses of the Legion of Honour, baronies, counties, *majorats*. It was an especial luck for a regiment to be received by the Emperor. But this practice was egregiously unjust. I could mention regiments which saw the Emperor four or five times in the course of a campaign; their officers were promoted every month; whereas, other regiments, detached to the distance of a couple of leagues, received no token whatever of the imperial munificence.

Napoleon sometimes took it into his head to question the officers, and when they answered without hesitation he appeared highly pleased. After the battle of Ratisbon, he stopped before an officer of my regiment.

"How many men present under arms?"

"Sire, eighty-four."

"How many conscripts of this year?"

"Twenty-two."

"How many soldiers who have served four years?"

"Sixty-five."

"How many wounded yesterday?"

"Eighteen."

"And killed?"

"Ten."

"With the bayonet?"

"Yes, sire."

"Good."

In order to be regularly killed, it was necessary to be killed with the bayonet: a coward may fall at a distance, struck by a bullet or a cannon-ball; whereas he who dies by the thrust of a bayonet must of course be a brave man. The Emperor showed especial tenderness for those who perished in this manner. He would continue his questions a long time on all sorts of petty details, and scarcely listen to the answers, the figures in which were often far from agreeing with previous statements: the main point was to give them off-hand, and without hesitation.

The Emperor Paul, of Russia, whom I am far from comparing with Napoleon, when he held a review, was accustomed to put to his officers the strangest and most absurd questions, which it was impossible for them to answer seriously. Several officers of one regiment, puzzled by these questions, had been put to a nonplus; and from that time the Emperor always said that those gentlemen belonged to his *know-nothing* regiment.

One day, riding on horseback over one of the bridges in St. Petersburg, Paul I. was met by an officer, who stopped and saluted him with due respect. The Emperor recognized the uniform. "This man belongs to my *know-nothing* regiment," said he to his courtiers.

"Ah, sire!" replied the officer, "but I know everything."

"Soho! you know everything, do you? we shall see. How many nails did it take to fasten the planks of this bridge?"

"Fifty-three million, nine hundred and seventy-nine thousand, one hundred and twelve."

"Not amiss! And how many fish are there in the Neva from this bridge to Cronstadt?"

"Six hundred and forty-two billion, eight hundred and one million, four hundred and thirty-two thousand, three hundred and seventy-nine."

"Are you quite sure of that?"

"Quite sure, or I should not tell your majesty so."

"Well, so I thought. I like to have answers to questions; an officer ought to know everything."

"Certainly; and the Emperor?"

"He is never at a loss."

"Will your Majesty deign to allow me one question?"

"Speak."

"What is my name?"

"Count de Balowski."

"My rank?"

"Captain in my guards."

"Many thanks to your Majesty."

I had this anedote from a French emigrant, an eye-witness of the circumstance, and acquainted with the sub-lieutenant Krasanow, who thus became, through sheer effrontery and the caprice of the sovereign, count and captain in the Russian imperial guard.

The Emperor Napoleon was often known to take off his cross of the Legion of Honour, and place it with his own hands on the bosom of a brave man. Louis XIV. would first have inquired if this brave man was noble. Napoleon asked if the noble was brave. A sergeant, who had performed prodigies of valour in a battle, was brought before Louis XIV. "I grant you a pension of twelve hundred livres," said the King.—"Sire, I should prefer the cross of St. Louis."—"I dare say you would, but you shall not have it." Napoleon would have hugged this sergeant; Louis XIV. turned his back on him: what a difference between the two periods!

In 1815, a high and mighty noble belonging to the court was nominated grand-cordon of the Legion of Honour. He considered this as an insult. Twenty conventicles were held in the noble faubourg, to decide whether he should refuse it. The party durst not affront Louis XVIII., but a middle course was steered. It was resolved that Bonaparte's ribbon should be worn on high days only, when etiquette absolutely required it. This decision was entirely in the spirit of Louis XIV.

Napoleon had a superb head, and eyes which flashed lightning; his attitude was noble and severe. One day, however, I saw the great man in the convulsions of inextinguishable laughter, for an emperor can laugh like any other man. Sovereigns, indeed, would be greatly to be pitied, if at times they had not those occasions for laughter which do one so much good.

The fact was this. We were at Courbevoie. The Emperor was reviewing a regiment of the young guard, which had recently been reinforced by numerous conscripts. His Majesty questioned one of these young men. "And you, where do you come from?" said Napoleon to the left-hand neighbour of a friend of mine, then sub-lieutenant, now receiver-general. "Sire," replied the conscript, "I come from Pezenas, and my father had the honour to shave your Eminence, when you passed through our place."

At these words the Emperor became man, decorum was forgotten, and I do not think that Napoleon ever laughed so heartily, even while at the school of Brienne. Laughter is contagious; the review terminated merrily; the expression flew from rank to rank; from right to left, every one was bursting; and the native of Pezenas was proud of having been the maker of so much mirth.

All sovereigns are fond of reviews. Frederick II. of Prussia sent tickets of invitation, and each had his precise place, good or bad, allotted to him by the King. Napoleon made less ceremony: all who chose came, and found places where they could. Certainly one of the finest reviews ever held in this world was that which the Emperor got up at Tilsit, where Alexander and Frederick-William figured by the side of Napoleon.

The Queen of Prussia was present at this review. Some years afterwards Canova chiselled her statue lying upon her tomb at Charlottenburg. I saw the lovely Queen Louisa at two different periods; the first time on horseback, radiant with health and youth; the second, extended on a superb sarcophagus, with marble drapery, marble hair; she was still very beautiful. If the living prove their affection for the dead by a magnificent tomb, certainly the King of Prussia has done for his consort all that it was possible to do. You cannot imagine an edifice in a purer style; it is a masterpiece of its kind.

That of the great Frederick at Potsdam is more simple, nay, it may be said, quite plain. In fact, the name of Frederick II., inscribed upon a tomb, says all that needs be known. What signifies it whether this inscription be engraven on marble or on gold? The name of Napoleon on a stone in St. Helena will outlast the pyramids of Egypt, which enclose unknown corses.

But here I have led you, before I was aware of it, from the plains of Tilsit to the vaults of Potsdam. Since we are there, and we have time, I will relate to you the history of the man who showed me the latter. He had formerly been an hussar; he assured me that he had lived familiarly with Frederick; if he spoke of that great man with admiration, I replied with enthusiasm, for the purpose of drawing out my cicerone, who was not backward to gratify my curiosity.

My hussar had fought in the field of Rosbach, and that name was incessantly occurring in his narrative: whenever he uttered it, an arch smile moved his old white moustaches, and a sidelong glance which he gave me betrayed gratified vanity. This name of Rosbach was his general date, his point of departure. Such a circumstance happened a year before Rosbach, two years after Rosbach: you would have thought, that this word, repeated so often before the tomb of Frederick, must have compensated his manes for the presence of a soldier of Napoleon's. While chatting, I happened to say that Rosbach was not very far from Jena, but I was sorry for it, for my poor hussar was quite disconcerted by the remark.

"You see this tomb," said he: "every day I mourn him who lies in it. Well, sir, if this great king were yet living, I should be still in prison—and would to God he were alive!—I should wish it even at the price of my liberty, of my life."

"And why should you be in prison?"

"Because I was shut up in the fortress of Spandau four years by his orders. I was not released till the accession of his nephew in 1786. Ah! would to God that I were yet between four walls, and could see through the bars of my window my good Fritz on his white charger, giving chase in the distance to your . . . . . Napoleon!"

He made a pause before he pronounced that name: he was on the point of prefixing to it some abusive epithet; the first syllable of the word *verfluchten* (cursed) even escaped him, but he stopped short.

"What had you done," said I, "to cause the King to confine you in Spandau?"

"I will tell you. Frederick had for his particular service an hussar, who lived in a small room situated under his closet. It was his duty to carry the King's letters at any minute of the night or day: a bell placed near the King's bed summoned him to receive orders. This hussar was selected from among the old soldiers, who were incapable of farther military service, and an excellent place he had. The King gave him nothing: he preferred making those to whom he wrote pay the porterage of his letter.* Each of

---

* All letters and petitions addressed to Frederick, to his ministers, and to persons in office, were required to be sent by post, and the postage paid: this produced at least one hundred thousand dollars per annum—a hint to ministers, present and future.

them was worth eight good groschen" (about a shilling) " to the hussar: that was the rate, and he durst not take more. Either from distrust, or some other reason, Frederick had made it a first consideration that this hussar should not be able to read.

"I had been severely wounded in the last campaign in Silesia; this was fifteen years after the battle of Rosbach, where, you know, we gave the French such a drubbing. The King knew me: he knew the name of every soldier in his army. At one of his reviews, when he was distributing rewards, he perceived me: my colonel spoke for me, and I was appointed his messenger. The King first asked me if I could read. Aware of the condition, yet wishing for the place, I answered No. You will hear what was the consequence of this untruth.

"While I was in the King's service, I saved a great deal of money; sometimes I had to deliver a hundred letters a day; for you must know that Frederick himself invited the people of distinction to his reviews, and assigned to each the place he was to occupy. I received so many eight good groschen pieces, that I grew rich; I had thoughts of obtaining my discharge and marrying. My duty began to seem irksome to me: when I was not trotting about the town, I was required to be in attendance, listening for the bell; and when a man knows that he has scraped together enough to keep him, he only wishes for opportunity to enjoy it. I had, therefore, a sweetheart; and we were waiting for a favourable occasion to ask the King's permission to marry— for old Fritz was not to be spoken to at all times.

"One day, when the King was to have gone out, I had agreed to meet my mistress: he was taken suddenly ill, and issued counter-orders. I sat down to write to my intended, and to apprise her of the circumstance. I had just begun my letter, when something or other called me away from my room. The King rang his bell; no hussar: he rang again, still no hussar. Upon this, old Fritz, in his morning-gown, sallies from his closet, comes down stairs all alone with the assistance of his crutch-stick, enters my room, finds my letter begun, and reads it. What I had written was this: such things one never forgets: 'My dear friend, I cannot call to see you this evening, because the old bear is ill . . .'

"Frederick went back to his cabinet. Presently afterwards he rang, and I attended the summons.

"'Hark ye,' said he, 'I want a discreet person, who may be entirely relied on; can I depend on you?'

"'Yes, sire, what are your commands?'

"'I want somebody to write a letter of the utmost importance, and wish that party to whom it will be addressed not to know from whom it comes. Everybody is acquainted with the handwriting of my secretaries; nobody knows yours; sit down, I will dictate to you.'

"'Your majesty forgets that I cannot write.'

"'Ah, yes; so you said to get your place—one of those white lies, which benefit the one, without injuring the other.'

"'Sire . . . . I assure you . . . .'

"'That you told a lie, then, and are telling one now.'

"'Indeed . . . .'

"'Not another word! here, take this pen, and write.'

"'Since your majesty insists upon it.'

"'*My dear friend.*'

"'*My dear friend,*' said I, when I had written it. A shudder began to come over me.

"'*I cannot call to see you this evening.*'

"At these words I turned pale, I trembled; I had not a drop of blood in my veins. The king repeated: '*I cannot call to see you this evening. Have you done?'

"'Yes, sire.'

"'*Because the old bear is ill*'—and the king laid particular emphasis on '*the old bear.*'

"'Forgive me, sire, forgive me!' said I, throwing myself at his feet.

"'Go on,' said he, ordering me to return to my seat; *because the old bear is ill, and I am at Spandau.*'

"I was obliged to write, sign, seal, and address the letter, and was immediately taken to my prison. There I should be still if the king had not died, for he was not very forgiving. I had deserved my punishment, and I did not complain. After four years' confinement, it was a grievous stroke to me to learn that I was going to recover my liberty because Frederick was no more. I loved him with all my soul, though I had taken the liberty to call him *the old bear*; it was a name that my sweetheart and I gave him between ourselves, though I would gladly have sacrificed my own life to lengthen his. Now that I am old, I show strangers the tomb in which that great king lies. I never enter these vaults without shedding tears; and the only ambition that I feel, an ambition that cannot be gratified, is to have a place here when I am dead."

Thus spoke my hussar of Rosbach. On leaving him, I slipped into his hand an eight good groschen piece. It called up recollections which moistened his eyes; and in the evening, on returning to Berlin, the first thing I did was to commit this anecdote to my tablets, from which I have here transcribed it.

CHAPTER XI.

MILITARY EXECUTIONS.

THE military laws are extremely severe: they must be so, otherwise how could a general enforce obedience from one hundred thousand men, each of whom individually is as strong as himself? A mere misdemeanour, which, in civil life, is punished with a few days' imprisonment, entails the penalty of death on the soldier. The least violence to a superior, the most trifling thing stolen from an enemy, costs the life of a man. The latter offence was punished only by fits and starts: for a fortnight or three weeks, the soldiers were allowed to rob as they pleased, because there were no provisions to distribute. If a few waggon-loads of bread or biscuit arrived, an order of the day immediately forbade every kind of pillage, and the first wretched wight taken in the fact suffered for all. I have seen many of these petty robbers shot for stealing a shirt or a pair of boots from a peasant; but never was a robber on a large financial scale visited with the slightest punishment. Sometimes the emperor made them disgorge, but they were never shot.

Military executions were only for the small fry. The laws are like spiders' webs; the fly is caught, the humble-bee breaks through them. The day before the battle of Wagram, twelve clerks of the victualling department were taken in the fact selling the rations of the imperial guard; they were shot a few hours afterwards.

These worthy clerks of the victualling department were really the prebendaries of the army. While the military portion of it fought and bivouacked in the mud, these gentry strutted about in the nearest villages, paying court to the ladies, at the same time that they stowed away in the magazines the flour furnished by the requisitions. They had in general more money than they knew what to do with. They could not send it to France by post, but in small quantity. If the sum had been too large, it would have attracted notice, and given rise to conjectures. The minister-at-war, on calculating that with a salary of one hundred louis it was not possible to save ten thousand francs per annum, would have dismissed the thief. They durst not leave the hoard at their quarters, for doors may be opened or forced. To keep it constantly about their persons was inconvenient, troublesome. Poor fellows! all of them took this latter course. I have seen some who carried an enormous weight around their waists, and whose garments were a cuirass of gold, placed between the cloth and the lining.

Differing in this respect from the usurers of Paris, who make young men accept bills for twice the amount that they give them, these *employés* offered a premium of 30 or 40 per cent. for the bills of officers who had wealthy relatives. Officers of my acquaintance have received 1500 francs in gold for a bill of exchange for 1000, payable in six months in France. The main point for these people was to secure their money: such a premium was to them of no real consequence: in three days they had made up for it.

He was certainly no fool who first conceived the idea of placing glory in the profession of arms: without this vehicle not a creature would follow it; nay, it is astonishing that any one will at that price. Suppose a man, organized as we are, were to come from the moon, and to be told: " Yonder are one hundred thousand men, who are going to fight at the command of an individual for interests which they know nothing about, and which not one of them cares about. Some go by force, others voluntarily; but all take a pride in running into the greatest possible dangers. They will get themselves killed, perhaps mutilated, crippled, which is frequently worse than death. They will endure all privations. all fatigues, all the inclemency of the weather. If any of these men disobeys his commander, he will be put to death; nay, more, his comrades will be his executioners. While these hundred thousand men are out of their country, striving to pick a quarrel with their neighbours, those who are left at home have to work to support them, to clothe them, and above all to supply the enormous waste for which war always furnishes a pretext. The hundred thousand men will come back wounded, racked with pains, in rags; and, by way of reward, they will be permitted to admire the statue of their general erected in some public place."

What would the man from the moon say to this? why, he would laugh outright in your face, and declare that it was impossible. A whole population would reply: "And yet it is nothing but the truth." Compelled to believe, he would then imagine that this general must possess such prodigious bodily strength as to fill all with terror. But what would he say on beholding a man bedizened with ribbon, who would not be a match at fisticuffs for the lowest drum-boy? He would say, I verily believe he would say, that the inhabitants of the earth are fools, and that their sovereigns are arrant knaves.

On seeing so many brave fellows knocking one another on the head, I could not help saying sometimes to myself: After all, this contempt of life under certain circumstances is a most singular thing in man. How happens it that those fellows who yesterday grumbled, cursed, swore, while executing a very simple order, the consequences of which were at most to make them go a league or two farther than there was occasion for—how happens it that they do not grumble to-day, when their lives are to be staked at odd or even? Because dishonour has been placed very far from grumbling, and very near to cowardice. Who then first took it into his head to mark these limits? He who had the strongest arm and the hardest fist: he beat the others; he insisted on their honouring him. "It is very agreeable to be honoured," said these others; "we have been beaten; let us beat our neighbours, and force them in their turn to pay us respect."

In some Arabian tale or other, we are told that a prince possessed an enchanted ring, which rendered the wearer invisible when it was turned. What would be the consequence, thought I, if, on a day of battle, each of us, Frenchman, Prussian, or Russian, had such a ring on his finger? I verily believe that at the first cannon-shot every one of us would turn his ring. I am there because you are there, and because you know that I am and ought to be there; but devil take me if I would stay there if you knew nothing about it!

When there is fighting in the night, people are not so particular; in the first place, because they see nothing themselves, and in the next, because they are not seen. Do you suppose that the brave Bianchelli, who led the assault of Tarragona, would have displayed such intrepidity if he had not been certain to attract the notice of a whole army?

A regiment is on march: the men are chatting, laughing aloud, singing jovial songs, keeping up a rolling fire of jokes and gibes. An aide-de-camp comes up: he speaks to the colonel, who gives orders to halt, and to load arms. Presently they resume their march; the jokes have ceased; not a word is spoken: each makes his reflections *in petto* on what is about to happen: there, man is alone with himself. The enemy makes his appearance; every one cries, Forward! every one is for dashing on at a run: there is man in contact with man. Are you for doing this? so will I—are you for running? well, I will get before you; but if you stop and seat yourself, I should like nothing better than to lie down.

I observed just now that it is only flies that are caught in cobwebs. At the time of the retreat from Portugal, General D—————— ordered a poor fellow to be shot for eating a bunch of grapes. "How horrible!" some will cry. "It is impossible!" exclaim others. It is most true, I reply; nay more, it was just. The dysentery was raging in the army; the soldiers were dying by dozens. The men were forbidden to eat grapes, that fruit being solely the cause of the disease. The first soldier caught in the fact paid for all the others. A council of war assembled by the way; a quarter of an hour afterwards the culprit had ceased to live.

What was the consequence? no more grapes were eaten, all recovered their health; by the sacrifice of one life several thousands were saved: the Commander-in-chief was right. It matters not whether D—————— had a right to issue this order, or whether he had not; this excessive severity was approved by all, for it saved perhaps half the army. Had some of those orators, with grandiloquent phrases, been there, certainly they would have had a wide field for the display of their eloquence; they would have obtained the pardon of the wretched wight; they would have caused the death of the body by sparing a limb. The death of the grape-eater was a necessity for all; it was requisite that every one should clearly perceive that the order of the day was not an empty threat; the moment each was convinced of this, the effect ceased from the cessation of the cause.

Had the like promptness been shown in enforcing the laws against the great robbers, the war in Spain would not have lasted so long. How many saints of gold and silver, how many pyxes and cups, were transformed into ingots, to be afterwards exchanged for hotels in Paris! How many diamonds and rubies, after adorning for ages the pompous and poetic ceremonies of the Roman Church, were utterly astonished to find themselves on the bare bosom of an opera-dancer!

The magnificent pictures which decorated the churches of Spain almost all found their way to France; they now adorn the galleries of the wealthy of our capital. In my time, there were scarcely any to be seen; we were shown the vacant places, covered by a piece of ignoble black serge; nothing was left but wretched representations of auto-da-fés, executed by the daubers of the Inquisition.

Had some of our amateurs of the fine arts, who protected them so efficiently in their baggage-waggons by a strong escort, been picked out, and shot, the war would not have become national; but then it would have been requisite that many persons should have given orders for their own execution.

These dilapidations were the cause of the war to the death which the Spaniards waged against us: thousands of soldiers were hanged because certain persons had plundered the churches and the convents. The priests and monks, seeing themselves robbed in a day of what they had been centuries in amassing, everywhere excited the people to insurrection; they made it the most sacred of duties; they devoted to everlasting flames all those who should not arm against the common enemy, and promised all the joys of paradise to such as should die in arms. In a country, where the minister of religion is always believed on his word, such a crusade, preached with the crucifix in one hand and a dagger in the other, could not fail to produce terrible results; and hence we ought not to be surprised at the prodigies which attended the siege of Saragossa.

But what I have ever disapproved, what was always a great affliction to me, was the severity with which pillage was punished one day, after it had been tacitly authorised for a month. From the moment the order was issued, wo betide him who disobeyed it! next day he was no more. When we arrived at Wismar, some soldiers went on a plundering excursion to the neighbouring villages; a peasant was killed: the maurauders were suddenly surrounded; two hundred were taken and confined in a church. General L—— immediately summoned a council of war, to try the murderer, who was to be shot next morning, before the departure of the division.

One of my friends, appointed reporter to the council, repaired to the church, followed by all the peasants: none of them could recognize the culprit, who probably had taken good care not to be caught. Our reporter hastened to the general, and stated the case.

"No matter," said General L——; "settle the matter as you please; the crime must be punished."

"Certainly! but who is to suffer?"

"That is your affair."

"The peasants all agree in declaring that the murderer has red epaulets—of course he must be a grenadier: now we have forty grenadiers among the prisoners; I ordered them to be separated from the others, but not one of them could be pointed out as the murderer."

"Put the names of all the grenadiers in a bag, and let him whose name is first drawn out, be shot to-morrow."

"General, I *cannot* undertake such an operation."

"I order you."

"I *will* not."

"Give me your sword."

"There it is."

"Take this captain to prison."

General L—— was at table. He rose in a rage, called the corporal of the guard, and ordered him to seize the captain-reporter. But, next morning, Philip fasting returned the sword, and nobody was shot.

In the vicinity of Bautzen, a voltigeur of my regiment was executed for robbing a woman of her black apron to make himself a cravat of it. The officers of his company besought General P—— to grant a reprieve till his pardon could be solicited of the Emperor: all was to no purpose; the poor fellow was shot. While the troops were coming upon the ground to attend the execution, some of the soldiers caught a leveret. The general went to them, and desired them to give him the animal. "Oh! what a pretty little creature! 'twere a pity to kill it!—so young too!" To save the poor thing from being strangled by the soldiers, the general galloped off, deposited the leveret in a place of safety, and then coolly returned to superintend the execution of his voltigeur.

A strange anomaly this to the observer. Here was a man scampering across rye-fields to seek an asylum for a leveret, who, a few minutes before, had been unmoved by the tears of an old captain begging the life of an old voltigeur. I have met here and there with persons whom Nature had endowed with a truly exquisite kind of sensibility.

A military execution is a terrible sight. I never witnessed a civil execution; I know nothing of the guillotine except from engravings; but my duty has frequently nailed me opposite to a wretched fellow-creature who was going to be shot. What the state of his pulse was I know not, but certainly his heart did not throb with greater violence than mine.

The troops form three sides of a square; the fourth is left vacant for the passage of the balls. Great military show is purposely made, and certainly with good reason; for since a terrible example is to be made, it ought to be rendered impressive to those who are left behind. The culprit arrives, accompanied by a priest. The drums all at once beat a march till the sufferer is in the centre of the troops. They then beat a *ban*, as that beat is called which precedes and follows every kind of proclamation. The captain-reporter reads the sentence, the drums close the ban; the culprit is made to kneel down; he is blindfolded, and twelve corporals, commanded by an adjutant-subaltern, fire at the wretched man at the distance of ten paces.

To diminish if possible, the agony, of the sufferer, the words of command are not uttered; the adjutant makes signals instead of them with his cane. In case the man is not killed outright, as it sometimes happens, a reserve platoon, composed of four men, is ready to despatch him by clapping the muzzles of their pieces to his head.

It is with an oppressed heart that I describe these horrors. Melancholy recollections crowd upon me: the wretched creatures, whom I have seen on their knees at this fatal moment, flit past me like phantoms: and yet, at all these executions, when they happened to take place near a town, some of the fair ladies belonging to it never failed to be present. With their delicate nerves, they made interest to obtain a place where they could have a good view; and then, next day, they were ill if a pullet was killed in their presence.

After the execution of the sentence, all the troops defile before the corpse. They then return to their quarters; the circumstance is talked of for two or three days, and very soon forgotten.

I have seen many of those unfortunate men die with admirable fortitude. I have seen some of them address the regiment, and give the command to fire, while not a syllable denoted the slightest emotion in them. But the man who, in this predicament, displayed the most astonishing courage was Malet. On being conducted, with twelve of his accomplices, to the plain of Grenelle, he, as the chief of the conspirators, asked permission to give the command to fire.

"Carry .... arms!" cried he, in a voice of thunder. "That won't do; we must begin again. Your piece on the arm, all of you! Carry .... arms! Good——Platoon .... arms! Present! Fire!" All fell excepting Malet; he was left standing alone. "And why not me, *sacré nom de Dieu!* .... Reserve platoon, forward! .... Right! Carry .... arms! Platoon .... arms! Present! Fire! ...."